Lead

as Jesus Led

BOOK 5   EXPERIENCE THE LIFE

Lead
as Jesus Led

Transformed Influence

BILL HULL & PAUL MASCARELLA

NAVPRESS

Discipleship Inside Out™

Discipleship Inside Out™

NavPress is the publishing ministry of The Navigators, an international Christian organization and leader in personal spiritual development. NavPress is committed to helping people grow spiritually and enjoy lives of meaning and hope through personal and group resources that are biblically rooted, culturally relevant, and highly practical.

For a free catalog go to www.NavPress.com
or call 1.800.366.7788 in the United States or 1.800.839.4769 in Canada.

ISBN-13: 978-1-61521-544-7

Cover design by Arvid Wallen
Cover image by Shutterstock

Printed in the United States of America

1 2 3 4 5 6 7 8 / 14 13 12 11 10

CONTENTS

INTRODUCTION

To *experience the life* is to commit to a way or pattern of life. Its basis is humility and it is a life of self-denial and submission to others. The life that Jesus lived and prescribed for us is different from the one being offered by many churches. His servant leadership was radically distinct from what is extolled by secular society and even too bold for what is modeled in the Christian community. This life is essentially the *faith of following*, of taking up one's cross daily and following Him. It is fundamentally about giving up the right to run your own life. It is living the life that Jesus lived, the life to which He has called every disciple.

To put it another way, we can only experience the life Jesus has called us to by committing to training that will enable us to believe as Jesus believed, live as Jesus lived, love as Jesus loved, minister as Jesus ministered, and lead as Jesus led.

It is only by taking Jesus' discipling yoke upon ourselves that we can experience the life that Jesus lived. Only then will we discover its light burden and enjoy His promised "rest for [our] souls" (Matthew 11:29-30).

ABOUT THIS BOOK

This book is the fifth in the five-book EXPERIENCE THE LIFE series. It continues the thirty-week course, built upon the ideas introduced and developed in Bill Hull's book *Choose the Life,* which begins with the series' first book, *Believe as Jesus Believed.*

Its Purpose

EXPERIENCE THE LIFE exists to assist the motivated disciple in entering into a more profound way of thinking and living. That way is the pattern of life Jesus modeled and then called every interested person to follow. Simply put, it is the living out of Jesus' life by: believing as Jesus believed, living as Jesus lived, loving as Jesus loved, ministering as Jesus ministered, and leading as Jesus led. This *Life* is a life grounded in humility—characterized by submission, obedience, suffering, and the joys of exaltation. It is the life that transforms its adherents and penetrates the strongest resistance. It then calls upon each person to rethink what it means to be a follower of Jesus.

This book is the fifth in the five-book EXPERIENCE THE LIFE series. It is designed to lead disciples in a thirty-week course, built upon the ideas introduced and developed in Bill Hull's book *Choose the Life.* It provides a daily format that directs a disciple's thinking toward the application of these truths, thereby producing in him a faith hospitable to healthy spiritual transformation—*a faith that embraces discipleship.*

Its Participants

Virtually all significant change can, should be, and eventually is tested in relationship to others. To say that one is more loving without its being verified in relation to others is hollow. Not only do others need to be involved to test one's progress, they are needed to encourage and help someone else in the journey of transformation. Therefore, going on the journey with others is absolutely necessary.

The five books are designed to lead each disciple in a personal journey of spiritual formation by participation within a community of disciples, who have likewise decided to *experience the life*.

The community is composed of (optimally) from two to six disciples being led in this thirty-week course to *experience the life*.

Participants in the community agree to make time and perform the daily assignments as directed in each book. They have agreed to pray daily for the other members of their community and to keep whatever is shared at their community meeting in confidence. They will attend and fully participate in each weekly community meeting.

Its Process

We recognize that all change, all spiritual transformation, is the result of a process. Events may instigate change in people; they may provide the motive, the occasion, and the venue for change to begin, but the changes that result in healthy spiritual transformation are the product of a process.

We can glean a description of the transformational process from the apostle Paul's command in Romans 12:2:

> Do not conform any longer to the pattern of this world, but be transformed by the renewing of your mind. Then you will be able to test and approve what God's will is—his good, pleasing and perfect will.

This process of transformation asserts that the believer must no longer conform to what is false, the "pattern of this world" (its ideas and values, and the behaviors that express them). Also, he must be transformed, which means his pattern must be changed, conformed to another pattern, (the truth), which is not "of this world." This is done by the process of "the renewing of your mind." What does it mean to renew something? To what is Paul referring when he says that the mind must undergo this renewal?

To renew something means to act upon something in ways that will cause it to be as it was when it was new. The principle idea is one of restoring something that is currently malfunctioning and breaking down to its fully functioning state, its original pristine state, the state it was in prior to its sustaining any damage. We must avoid the modern notion that renewing something means simply replacing the old thing with an entirely new thing. Paul, and the people to whom he wrote these words, would simply not understand *renew* to mean anything like what we moderns mean when we use the word *replace*. They would understand that renewing the wheels on one's cart meant repairing them to their fully functioning state. And so, what Paul means by "being transformed by the *renewing* of your mind" (emphasis ours) is that the mind must undergo changes, repairs that will restore it to its original condition, the fully functioning state it enjoyed when it was first created. As these repairs proceed in the restoration/renewal process and a detrimental modification to the original design is discovered, that modification must be removed. It must be removed so that it will not interfere with its operating as it was originally designed. Further, to properly renew anything, we must understand its original design. The best way to renew something is with the direction and assistance of the original builder. A builder in Paul's day was not only the builder but also the designer and architect. With the expertise and help available through the builder, full renewal is best accomplished.

If you are renewing a house, that house's builder would best know how to go about it. If you are renewing an automobile, that automobile's builder would best know how to go about it. In our case, we are renewing the mind. It stands to reason, then, that its renewal would best be accomplished in partnership with its Architect/Builder — God.

We know that it is the mind that is to be renewed, and that we should partner with God to accomplish its renewal, but what is it about the mind that is being renewed? Is it broken, in need of new parts?

When Paul says that it is the mind which is being renewed when spiritual transformation is taking place, he means much more than what most of us think of when we use the word *mind*. Most of us think of the mind as some sort of calculator in our head, so, it's understandable that our idea of renewing it would start with the idea of replacing its broken parts. But for Paul, the mind is much more than a calculator in our head, and to renew it means more than simply swapping out a sticky key, or a cracked screen, or replacing the batteries that have run low.

The Greek word that Paul uses and is translated as the English word *mind* is νους. Here it means the inner direction of one's thoughts and will and the orientation of one's moral consciousness. When Paul refers to our mind's renewal, he is saying that the current direction of our thoughts and will must be changed. The way our mind currently directs our thoughts and will no longer leads to where the mind was originally designed to take our thoughts and will. Our mind no longer leads our thinking to know the will of God, to know what is good, pleasing, and perfect, and no longer directs our will to accomplish God's will, to do what is good, pleasing, and perfect. This is in large part what is meant by being lost. If our minds are not renewed, then we cannot live a life directed toward doing what is pleasing to God. We need to undergo the restoration process that will return our minds to operating as they were originally designed, allowing our minds to direct our thinking and will toward God. The good news is that the original Builder/Architect—God—prescribed the renewing of the mind as the sure remedy to restoring us to spiritual health, and He intends to partner with us in this restoration process.

For spiritual transformation to occur there must be a partnership between the Holy Spirit and the person who is to undergo transformation. It is good news that the Holy Spirit is involved in the process of our restoration because, unlike other things that undergo restoration, like houses, tables, and chairs, we are not just passive things. We are more. We are *beings*, *human* beings, *made* in the image of God. Being made in the image of God includes much more than I will (or even can) mention, but for our purposes it includes having thoughts, ideas, passions, desires, and a will of our own. Because these abilities in their current condition (i.e., before renewal) no longer lead us toward God's will, we do not have the ability to direct our own transformation. We need someone who is not "conformed to the pattern of this world," one who is completely conformed to the will of God, to direct the renewal. And because we are in this prerenewal condition, we need someone to initiate, to enable us, and encourage us to continue the process, someone who is not subject to the same problems our condition allows. Who is better to direct than God? Who is better to enable and encourage than God? There is none better suited to the task than the Holy Spirit. That we are partnering with Him is good news indeed!

With the initiating, enabling, and direction of the Holy Spirit, the process of renewal can begin. It is a two-stage process: the *appropriation of the truth* and the *application of truth-directed behavior*. The first stage, the *appropriation of the truth* takes place when:

1. We have the desire to pursue the Truth to be changed;
2. We then act upon that desire, choosing to pursue the Truth by setting our will.

The second stage, the *application of truth-directed behavior* takes place when:

1. We begin practicing behaviors, which we'll describe as spiritual disciplines, designed to halt our conformity to "the pattern of this world";
2. We engage in transformational activities, which are designed to reorient our mind and direct it toward God's will;
3. We continue to practice transformational activities to introduce and establish new patterns of thinking and behavior which conforms our mind to the mind of Christ.

The same components in the process for renewing the mind that we gleaned from the apostle Paul can also be seen in Jesus' call to anyone who would follow Him.

Jesus commanded to all who would follow Him (all disciples) to:

Come to me, all you who are weary and burdened, and I will
give you rest. Take my yoke upon you and learn from me, for I
am gentle and humble in heart, and you will find rest for your
souls. (Matthew 11:28-29)

Jesus begins with a promise, "Come . . . and I will give you rest." He
kindles a desire to follow Him. This is the first step in *the appropriation
of truth*, the *desire* to pursue the Truth. We *desire* change. Next is Jesus'
command to take His yoke. This is the second step in the *appropriation
of truth*, *choosing* to pursue the truth. We set our *will* to change. At this
step, we can choose to pursue our desire for the truth and change or
ignore it. If we choose to delay placing it upon our shoulders it is at the
cost of rest to our souls. The choice precedes the action. Next, we read
that we are to take His yoke.

To take His yoke is the first step of the second stage in the process
of renewing the mind, the *application of truth-directed behavior*. At this
step, as we saw before with Paul, we discontinue with our current ways,
which conform us to the pattern of this world. We intentionally begin
to dislodge the destructive patterns that have grown in us as a precursor
to the second step, the taking-upon of a new way, God's way, His yoke.

The second step, the taking-upon of Jesus' yoke, is the part of the
process of renewing the mind where the vacancy left from dislodging
our old ways, "the pattern of this world," is being filled up with the new
life-giving patterns by which we are to conform our lives. It is this yoke,
God's new way of living the life that Jesus lived, that is to be taken upon
us. Just as the yoke for an ox is placed upon its body, allowing the power
of the ox to perform its master's work (work the ox would otherwise
not be able to accomplish), so also Jesus' yoke must be placed upon our
body to allow it to perform our Master's work, the renewing of our mind
(work we would otherwise not be able to accomplish).

Finally, we see the third, and last step, in the *application of truth-
directed behavior*. This is the final step in the process of renewal, but it
is also the beginning step in the ongoing process of our spiritual transformation. It finally brings us all the way to our taking Jesus' yoke upon

us. It also begins the continuing journey of knowing and doing God's good, pleasing, and perfect will. While the second step trains the mind by establishing patterns, the third step lives out the new character that is replacing the old. This continuing journey begins once we take His yoke upon us. For then we begin to "learn from me [Jesus]" and thereby experience rest for our soul. This rest, this peacefulness that comes from learning from Jesus, is what it is to live with a renewed mind. It is experiencing the Spirit-initiated, encouraged, enabled, and empowered life Jesus enjoyed with the peace that comes only by having the "mind of Christ" and by accomplishing His good, pleasing, and perfect will.

EXPERIENCE THE LIFE provides the disciple a structured process whereby he can engage in the process of spiritual renewal. It provides a daily regimen for practicing specific disciplines designed to displace those old destructive ideas and behaviors (the patterns of the world) and replacing them with new, constructive, life-giving ideas and behaviors (the mind of Christ).

EXPERIENCE THE LIFE requires commitment to consistently practice the disciplines and to reserve the time required for transformation.

Most studies on change agree that displacing a current habit or idea and establishing a new one requires a minimum of about three months. Also, learning studies demonstrate the necessity of consistent application of the thing being learned to ensure its permanent retention.

According to a leading learning researcher, people remember:

- 10% of what they read
- 20% of what they hear
- 30% of what they see
- 50% of what they see and hear
- 70% of what they say
- 95% of what they teach someone else[1]

---

1. William Glassner, *Control Therapy in the Classroom* (New York: Harper and Row, 1986); *Reality Therapy: A New Approach to Psychiatry* (New York: Harper and Row, 1965).

Simply put, we learn best not by passively hearing and seeing, but by actively "doing" the thing which we are learning.

The most relevant question a teacher can ask is, "Are my students learning?" For our purposes, the relevant question must be, "Am I engaged in a process that will result in my being changed from what I am into what I am to be? Am I being transformed into the image of Christ?"

Each book in this series provides a solid opportunity for significant transformation through the use of several common tools or disciplines including:

- Reading Scripture together
- Reading a common philosophy of the Christian experience
- Journaling insights, questions, and prayers
- Discussion over material that has already been studied, prayed over, and reflected upon
- Accountability for the purpose of helping each other keep their commitments to God
- Encouragement to help each other overcome areas of defeat and break free of bondage
- Mutual commitment to apply what God has impressed on each member
- Mutual commitment to impact those with whom they have contact

Its Pattern

This course leads the believer to *experience the life* Jesus lived, utilizing a daily regimen to practice the various spiritual disciplines. The course is thirty weeks long over five books.

The five books, each six weeks in length, instruct and challenge the disciple to conform his life to:

1. Believe as Jesus believed,
2. Live as Jesus lived,
3. Love as Jesus loved,

4. Minister as Jesus ministered, and

5. Lead as Jesus led.

Each six-week book leads disciples through a course of daily teach-ings and exercises in an examination of how Jesus lived out his faith.

In five daily sessions, the disciple begins with a prayer focused on the issues to be presented in the daily reading. The daily reading gives a core thought that will be explored in the day's exercises. Questions are designed to help the disciple's understanding of the core thoughts and key ideas. Disciples are then directed to reflect on the application of these core thoughts and key ideas to their own spiritual growth. Journaling space is provided for answering questions and recording thoughts, ques-tions, applications, and insights stemming from their reflection.

Once weekly (the sixth session), the disciple meets with others who comprise their community. At the community meeting they pray together, discuss the core thoughts and key ideas introduced in the week's readings, and share from their own experience of practicing the week's spiritual discipline. They view and discuss the video introduc-tion for the following week's study and pray and encourage one another in their journey of spiritual transformation.

Although the books were designed primarily for use by groups consisting of two to six members, the material and the format can easily be used to effectively lead larger groups in a discussion-based exploration of spiritual transformation.

Lastly, we recommend that the leaders of the weekly discussion groups proceed through each book together as a community group prior to leading their own group. The insights that they will acquire from their own journey through EXPERIENCE THE LIFE will be invalu-able to them and the larger group they will lead.

When leading a larger group through EXPERIENCE THE LIFE, keep in mind that most of the spiritual traction for transformation is due to the interaction that the Lord has with each individual through the other individuals in a community of believers. To preserve this trac-tion, the leader must provide a venue and time for this interaction. For this reason, we suggest that some time during the weekly session, the leader divide the large group into smaller groups mimicking the two- to six-member community group for the purpose of more intimately discussing the issues presented in the week's session. It is reported after experiencing successive weeks with the same members of this smaller discussion group individuals previously not participants in a small-group program have desired to continue in such a program.

While we believe that the most effective and efficient means of leading individuals to healthy spiritual transformation is in the context of a smaller community group, we do acknowledge that the larger group setting may be the only means currently available to a church's leadership. Though the *form* of instruction is important, the *function* is what must be preserved: *Verum supremus vultus* (truth above form).

Its Product

Each session is designed to challenge the disciple to examine the progress of his own transformation, to train him with the desire to both know God's will and do it. This course values the spiritual traction the disciple can get by facing this challenge in a high-trust community. Christ was a Man for others. Disciples then are to be people for others. It is only in losing ourselves in the mission of loving others that we live in balance and experience the joy that Christ has promised. And therein lie many of the rewards a disciple may enjoy as he lives and loves as Jesus. This is the life that cultivates Christlikeness and whose product is a transformed disciple—the only life of faith worthy of justifying our calling upon others to EXPERIENCE THE LIFE.

WEEK ONE

Influence

DAY ONE

Prayer

Father, help me to use what You have taught me about You and what I am learning about myself to help others know You. Amen.

Core Thought

> A leader is someone who uses their power to influence a person's thoughts and actions to cause some kind of change in their thinking and behavior.

What is a leader? A leader is someone who uses their power to influence a person's thoughts and actions to cause some kind of change in their thinking and behavior. So then, a leader is someone who does two things: influences and causes change. This being true, the next question to be answered is, "Who does the Lord call to be a leader?"

The answer to this question is actually quite simple. As such, it is also easily confused. The Lord calls as leaders all those whom He has commanded to influence and cause change in people. And, of course, He has commanded all believers to do this.

All believers are commanded to think and act in ways that will influence the thoughts and actions of others. Jesus commanded us to be salt and light in this world and to act in such honorable ways that men will see our good works and give thanks to Him on the day He returns (Matthew 5:16). So then, is every Christian a leader? The astounding answer is yes!

Being a leader boils down to being someone the Lord uses to influence a person's thoughts and actions, to bring about the changes He desires to see in their character. Since God has called all Christians to be leaders, that leaves us with the important question, "How are we to lead?" We will begin to answer that question tomorrow as we discuss the kind of person God uses to lead others.

Today's Exercises
Core Scripture: 1 Peter 2:9-12
Read aloud 1 Peter 2:9-12.
Recite this week's memory verse aloud five times.

> And the things you have heard me say in the presence of many witnesses entrust to reliable men who will also be qualified to teach others. (2 Timothy 2:2)

Meditate on today's passage.

Request to Be in His Presence
"Dear Lord, bring me into the context of Your world."

1. **Read it**—Remember: We read now only what is there, to hear once again, only what was spoken then. Read 2 Timothy 1:1-4 at least twice, out loud.
2. **Think it**—select a portion, a phrase within the reading, and mull it over in your mind, thinking about the context and setting, reimagining the event, putting yourself into the situation. As you meditate, use all five senses to re-create the context and the setting by building the images that are supplied within the passages.
3. **Pray it**—ask God to give you understanding into how the truths He has spoken in these Scriptures apply to you now. Ask, "What is it about me that I need to deal with? What is it about me that must change?"

Respond to God by accepting and admitting whatever responsibility is implied by what He has shown. Write what it is that God has shown you, and what you must admit responsibility for having done (or not done).

4. ***Live it***—ask God to reveal to you what He wants you to do about what you have admitted.

State what God has revealed that you must admit responsibility for doing.

State what particular action(s) you will take today to accomplish what God has revealed for you to do.

Discovering the Discipline: Silence and Solitude

Leaders don't always appreciate what we need the most, but God knows. When we change our basic mode of operation from the belief that our hard work and strategies are what make things happen, it changes our core behavior. This reorganization requires that we begin with silence and solitude—the primary starting point for a leader who wants to be transformed by God and to lead others into the same experience.

The spiritual disciplines of solitude and silence go hand in hand. The discipline of solitude uses silence to amplify its power to reveal the issues hidden inside us that hinder us in becoming Christlike. The discipline of silence uses solitude to focus its power to release us from the things that bind us. We need to discover, understand, and become practiced in both disciplines to lead as Jesus led.

Today, we will begin our discovery by understanding what the spiritual discipline of solitude is and why it should be practiced.

Dallas Willard gives us a very workable definition of the spiritual discipline of solitude:

> By solitude we mean being out of human contact, being alone, and being so for lengthy periods of time. To get out of human contact is not something that can be done in a short while, for that contact lingers long after it is, in one sense, over. We have already seen what a large role solitude played in the life of our Lord and the great ones in His Way. In solitude, we purposely fully abstain from interaction with other human beings, denying ourselves companionship and all that comes from our conscious interaction with others. We close ourselves away; we go to the ocean, to the desert, the wilderness, or to the anonymity of the urban crowd. This is not just rest or refreshment from nature, though that too can contribute to our spiritual well-being. Solitude is choosing to be alone and to dwell on our experience of isolation from other human beings.[1]

Willard also helps us to understand why we should practice this discipline:

> Solitude frees us, actually. This above all explains its primacy and priority among the disciplines. The normal course of day-to-day human interactions locks us into patterns of feeling, thought, and action that are geared to a world set against God. Nothing but solitude can allow the development of a freedom from the ingrained behaviors that hinder our integration into God's order. . . . In solitude, we confront our own soul with its

---

1. Dallas Willard, *The Spirit of the Disciplines* (San Francisco: Harper & Row, 1992), 160.

obscure forces and conflicts that escape our attention when we are interacting with others. Of all the disciplines of abstinence, solitude is generally the most fundamental in the beginning of the spiritual life, and it must be returned to again and again as that life develops.[2]

Solitude is the basic spiritual discipline. Without it you will be hindered in everything else you try:

This practice breaks the back of self-sufficiency—the need to be in control and in the fray. If we give Jesus His way and follow His example, He will say, "Stop here first. Sit a while and let's get on the same page." God says, "Lie down here where it is quiet, where I can talk to you, where you can hear what I have to say." This is counterintuitive for the high achiever, so I want to affirm to all high achievers the truth that solitude is action! Henri Nouwen wrote that solitude is the furnace of transformation.[3]

Doing the Discipline: Silence and Solitude

You may be saying to yourself, "Practicing this silence and solitude stuff would be possible . . . if I were a monk! Can a normal person, with a family and a job, practice solitude and silence?" The answer is yes. There are believers who do. Throughout the remainder of this book, I will pass on some ways that normal believers have practiced solitude and silence in their daily lives.

Richard Foster suggests that the first thing we should do is take advantage of the little solitudes that fill our day:

Consider the solitude of those early morning moments in bed

---

2. Willard, 160–161.

3. Bill Hull, *Choose the Life: Exploring a Faith that Embraces Discipleship* (Grand Rapids, MI: Baker, 2006), 200.

before the family awakens. Think of the solitude of a morning cup of coffee before beginning the work of the day. There is the solitude of bumper-to-bumper traffic during the freeway rush hour. There can be little moments of rest and refreshment when we turn a corner and see a flower or a tree. Instead of vocal prayer before a meal, consider inviting everyone to join into a few moments of gathered silence. Once while driving a carload of chattering children and adults, I exclaimed, "Let's play a game and see if everyone can be absolutely quiet until we reach the airport" (about five minutes away). It worked, blessedly so. Find new joy and meaning in the little walk from the subway to your apartment. Slip outside just before bed and taste the silent night.

These tiny snatches of time are often lost to us. What a pity! They can and should be redeemed. They are times for inner quiet, for reorienting our lives like a compass needle. They are little moments that help us to be genuinely present where we are.[4]

Those brief, daily, little solitudes provide the greatest number of opportunities for experiencing the benefits of silence and solitude. For us normal folks, apart from these little solitudes, very little of the Lord's character could be grown in us, but for us to experience a full measure of those benefits there is no better way than to reserve occasions of extended time in solitude and silence with the Lord.

Practicing the Discipline of Solitude

Today, we will begin to practice the discipline of solitude. We will do so by taking some time each day to come apart from the usual running of our day to be with Him, to hear Him, and to be refreshed by Him.

We will also begin preparing for the one-day personal retreat dedicated to practicing the spiritual disciplines of silence and solitude. The

---

4. Richard Foster, *Celebration of Discipline* (New York: Harper and Row, 1978), 105–106.

retreat will take place on the fifth day of Week Six. It is planned to coincide with the last community meeting of the EXPERIENCE THE LIFE course. At that meeting, you will be sharing and summing up your experiences. It is important for you to make whatever arrangements are necessary to ensure that you will be able to participate on that day with all of your community members. This is why we have given this notice so long before the event.

Today, take the following steps.

1. Put the one-day personal retreat on your calendar.
2. Take a fifteen- to thirty-minute silent prayer walk.
   a. Walk alone.
   b. Select a place where you are not likely to be disturbed, somewhere safe and as pleasant as possible.
   c. As you walk, ask the Lord, "When today have I reacted when You would have preferred for me to be still? Why did I react?"
3. What were the Lord's answers to your questions?

Journal

Record ideas, impressions, feelings, questions, and any insights you may have had during today's time.

Prayer

Pray for each member of your community.

Influence

DAY TWO

Prayer

Dear Lord, train me to respond to others from the fullness of the depth of character You are growing in me instead of reacting to them out of the emptiness of my current shallow character. Grow me into someone in whom You are delighted. Amen.

Core Thought

> A leader is not so much the kind of person who has a particular kind of position as it is a kind person who has a particular kind of disposition.

Yesterday we defined a leader as someone the Lord uses to influence a person's thoughts and actions, to bring about the changes He desires to see in their character. We said that God has called all Christians to be leaders and that despite the simplicity of these two truths, there is still confusion as to what is meant by leading and being a leader in Christ's church.

The confusion arises from failing to understand that in Christ's church, all Christians are called to lead but only some are called to be organizational leaders within the church. *All* are called to be someone the Lord uses to influence a person's thoughts and actions, to bring about the changes He desires to see in their character. However, only *some* are called to serve as leaders in some official position or capacity, like senior pastor, elder, or as director of a particular ministry. This is the basis for the confusion.

Our culture has taught us that a leader is someone who has an official title, occupies an official position, and can exercise official powers and that a leader needs only one thing: official recognition. You can see by this definition that being a leader boils down to being someone with a title and a position. Leadership then is just another way of saying, "It's official, you have to do as I say . . . because unlike you, I am both qualified and entitled." This is the less abrupt way of saying, "I am your leader (and you must follow me) because I am better than you." But our culture has told us a lie about the kind of person it takes to be a leader.

A leader is not so much the kind of person who has a particular kind of position as it is a kind person who has a particular kind of disposition. In fact, when we look at Jesus, we see a Leader who makes our following Him desirable. We see His kindness. In fact what distinguishes Him from the other leaders (like the Pharisees, the Sadducees, and the scribes) is the fullness of His kindness to His followers.

Unlike other leaders, Jesus treats His followers with kindness. His manner of treating others is the perfect example of what it means to "do to others as you would have them do to you" (Matthew 7:12) and to "love your neighbor as yourself" (Matthew 22:39). Jesus is a kind person. But He is also a kind person with a particular kind of disposition.

The fullness of Jesus' kindness can be seen by His willingness to be fully identified with those who follow Him; He shows Himself to be "like our *kind*." He shows His kindness with us by being predisposed to dispensing with all the trappings that show His superiority to us. He puts aside all those things that demonstrate His own greatness for the sake of others. He becomes the same *kind* as we are, servants of God the Father. He does this in order to do before God what we are commanded but cannot ourselves do: offer ourselves perfectly to God for the sake of others.

Having this kind of disposition, one that "didn't think so much of himself that he had to cling to the advantages of that status no matter what,"[5] makes Him the expression of perfect *kind*-ness by being the

---

5. Eugene H. Peterson, *The Message: The Bible in Contemporary Language*, Philippians 2:6 (Colorado Springs, CO: NavPress, 2002).

first of our *kind*, the first of man*kind* to serve God perfectly by serving others (Philippians 2:7-8). He is the God-Man who serves God for man's sake.

To lead as Jesus led requires that we display the same fullness of kindness that Jesus has shown, kindness that the world rejects, kindness that treats others with the same loving care that we ourselves desire to experience, and kindness that shows that we are predisposed toward taking our position as God's servants, serving others. To lead as Jesus led requires that we become transformed leaders.

Today's Exercises

Core Scripture: 1 Peter 2:9-12
Read aloud 1 Peter 2:9-12.
Recite this week's memory verse aloud five times.

> And the things you have heard me say in the presence of many witnesses entrust to reliable men who will also be qualified to teach others. (2 Timothy 2:2)

Meditate on today's passage.

Request to Be in His Presence

"Dear Lord, bring me into the context of Your world."

1. ***Read it*** — Remember: We read now only what is there, to hear once again, only what was spoken then. Read 2 Timothy 1:5-7 at least twice, out loud.
2. ***Think it*** — select a portion, a phrase within the reading, and mull it over in your mind, thinking about the context and setting, reimagining the event, putting yourself into the situation. As you meditate, use all five senses to re-create the context and the setting by building the images that are supplied within the passages.
3. ***Pray it*** — ask God to give you understanding into how the truths He has spoken in these Scriptures apply to you now. Ask, "What

is it about me that I need to deal with? What is it about me that must change?"

Respond to God by accepting and admitting whatever responsibility is implied by what He has shown. Write what it is that God has shown you, and what you must admit responsibility for having done (or not done).

4. *Live it*—ask God to reveal to you what He wants you to do about what you have admitted.

State what God has revealed that you must admit responsibility for doing.

State what particular action(s) you will take today to accomplish what God has revealed for you to do.

Doing the Discipline: Silence and Solitude

Practicing the Discipline of Solitude

1. Inform your family about the one-day personal retreat.
2. Take a fifteen- to thirty-minute silent prayer walk.
   a. Walk alone.
   b. Select a place where you are not likely to be disturbed, some-where safe, quiet, and as pleasant as possible.

    c. As you walk, ask the Lord, "When today have I reacted when You would have preferred for me to be still? Why did I react?"

3. What were the Lord's answers to your questions?

Journal

Record ideas, impressions, feelings, questions, and any insights you may have had during today's time.

Prayer

Pray for each member of your community.

Influence

DAY THREE

Prayer

Dear Lord, help me to understand what You mean about being a leader
and about what it is You expect me to do as a leader. Amen.

Core Thought

> Transformed leaders are the Holy Spirit's tool for
> spreading God's transforming influence within the church.

Previously, we have asked and answered the questions, "What is a
leader?" and "What kind of person does God use to lead others?" We
learned that a leader is someone who brings about change by initiating
changes in other people's thinking and behavior. We also learned that
God uses believers who are becoming predisposed to serving others
(transformed leaders) and whose manner shows the loving care that
Jesus demonstrated as He served others. Today, we will begin to answer
the question of who God's leaders are to lead.

"Who do God's transformed leaders lead?" is best answered by
first understanding whose character God intends to transform through
the influence of His transformed leaders. The answer is the world, all
people of every nation, the world that God loved so much so that He
gave for it His only begotten Son so that any of its people who believe
in His Son will have everlasting life. While this answers the question
of who, it leaves the question as to how God will influence the world.

The way God has chosen to spread His transforming influence
upon the world is through a select people, the church, whom He

prepares for this task. In order for the world to receive God's transforming influence, it first must be delivered by the believers within the church. The way God prepares the church to deliver is by spreading this same transforming influence within the church. He does this through transformed leaders.

Transformed leaders are the Holy Spirit's tool for spreading God's transforming influence within the church. It is a truism that "one cannot give to others what one does not himself possess." So for the church to spread God's transforming influence to the world, its members must be transformed carriers. Otherwise, we have no power within us to transform, and therefore, at best, the influence we have will only bring about damaging deformities in the character of others. Likewise, if the church you attend is comprised of members who remain untransformed . . . well, you get the picture. You probably know better than others that the influence being spread by such a church is almost inconsequential. But this is not what Christ desires for His church.

It can only be through God's transforming influence, delivered by His transformed leaders, that ineffective and inconsequential churches will be transformed into ones against which the gates of hell cannot prevail.

For the gates to fall, the church must prevail. To prevail it must have within it God's transforming power. To overcome the world and reach the lost for Christ, it must deliver God's transforming influence out of the reservoirs of its transformed leaders.

Today's Exercises
Core Scripture: 1 Peter 2:9-12
Read aloud 1 Peter 2:9-12.
Recite this week's memory verse aloud five times.

> And the things you have heard me say in the presence of many witnesses entrust to reliable men who will also be qualified to teach others. (2 Timothy 2:2)

Meditate on today's passage.

Request to Be in His Presence
"Dear Lord, bring me into the context of Your world."

1. ***Read it***—Remember: We read now only what is there, to hear once again, only what was spoken then. Read 2 Timothy 1:11-14; 2:1-2 at least twice, out loud.

2. ***Think it***—select a portion, a phrase within the reading, and mull it over in your mind, thinking about the context and setting, reimagining the event, putting yourself into the situation. As you meditate, use all five senses to re-create the context and the setting by building the images that are supplied within the passages.

3. ***Pray it***—ask God to give you understanding into how the truths He has spoken in these Scriptures apply to you now. Ask, "What is it about me that I need to deal with? What is it about me that must change?"

    Respond to God by accepting and admitting whatever responsibility is implied by what He has shown. Write what it is that God has shown you, and what you must admit responsibility for having done (or not done).

4. ***Live it***—ask God to reveal to you what He wants you to do about what you have admitted.

State what God has revealed that you must admit responsibility for doing.

State what particular action(s) you will take today to accomplish what God has revealed for you to do.

Doing the Discipline: Silence and Solitude

Practicing the Discipline of Solitude

1. Inform your work or other responsibilities about the one-day personal retreat.
2. Take a fifteen- to thirty-minute silent prayer walk.
   a. Walk alone.
   b. Select a place where you are not likely to be disturbed, somewhere safe, quiet, and as pleasant as possible.
   c. As you walk, ask the Lord, "When today have I reacted when You would have preferred for me to be still? Why?"
3. What were the Lord's answers to your questions?

Journal

Record ideas, impressions, feelings, questions, and any insights you may have had during today's time.

Prayer

Pray for each member of your community.

Influence

DAY FOUR

Prayer

Dear Lord, I may have misunderstood or was mistaught the way You wanted to use me to bring the gospel to others. Please teach me and help me to dislodge anything that is not right in my understanding about the message and the way You want the gospel communicated to the lost. Train me to replace it with its transforming truth. Amen.

Core Thought

> Transformed leaders are the Holy Spirit's tool for spreading God's transforming influence throughout the world.

The target of God's transforming influence is huge. It is the world. God has chosen to transform its people by first transforming the people of His own kingdom. As God uses His people to lead one another in forming Christ's character within them, He uses them as tools for spreading His transforming influence throughout the world.

As we are being transformed through the renewing of our mind and the disciplining of our behaviors and as our character is being conformed to Christ's within the safe confines of the fellowship of other believers, God is building within us a vast reservoir of transforming power. He intends to loose from these reservoirs His transforming power onto all those in our sphere of influence, where we live, work, and play. He will use our accessibility to others as His means for making Himself accessible for others.

Though it is not exclusively so, it is clearly God's preference that those who do not as yet believe in Him should come to know of and about Him and begin to experience His love for them through their interactions with believers.

Today, because of the disobedience of one man, no man may encounter God directly as he once did when he walked with Him in the garden long ago. Our father Adam's disobedience brought guilt, shame, and condemnation upon the whole family of man. From Adam's day forward, though they may not recognize it as such, all men continue to experience the feeling of irreconcilable isolation from the God who loves them. But it was always God's plan to provide the way of reconciliation.

God's plan was that He Himself would return mankind to Himself. The perfect Son of God would become the perfect Son of Man, Jesus. Through His perfect obedience to His Father's will, He reconciled mankind to God. Today, Jesus continues His ministry of reconciling the world to God. He does so through the believers that comprise His church. And all is going according to plan.

As those who have not yet believed in Christ and been reconciled to God witness the love that exists between believers who are being transformed into Christ's image (John 13:34-35) and as they begin to experience His kindness and love through their encounters with those transformed leaders, they will be swept away by these streams of living water (John 7:38) and carried to the Rock who is Jesus (1 Corinthians 10:4) from whom this River of Life flows (Revelation 22:1).

Today's Exercises

Core Scripture: 1 Peter 2:9-12

Read aloud 1 Peter 2:9-12.

Recite this week's memory verse aloud five times.

> And the things you have heard me say in the presence of many witnesses entrust to reliable men who will also be qualified to teach others. (2 Timothy 2:2)

Meditate on today's passage.

Request to Be in His Presence

"Dear Lord, bring me into the context of Your world."

1. ***Read it***—Remember: We read now only what is there, to hear once again, only what was spoken then. Read 1 Peter 1:3 at least twice, out loud.
2. ***Think it***—select a portion, a phrase within the reading, and mull it over in your mind, thinking about the context and setting, reimagining the event, putting yourself into the situation. As you meditate, use all five senses to re-create the context and the setting by building the images that are supplied within the passages.
3. ***Pray it***—ask God to give you understanding into how the truths He has spoken in these Scriptures apply to you now. Ask, "What is it about me that I need to deal with? What is it about me that must change?"

   Respond to God by accepting and admitting whatever responsibility is implied by what He has shown. Write what it is that God has shown you, and what you must admit responsibility for having done (or not done).
4. ***Live it***—ask God to reveal to you what He wants you to do about what you have admitted.

State what God has revealed that you must admit responsibility for doing.

State what particular action(s) you will take today to accomplish what God has revealed for you to do.

Doing the Discipline: Silence and Solitude

Practicing the Discipline of Solitude

1. Determine where you will have the one-day personal retreat:
    a. Select a quiet place where you will not be disturbed.
    b. You will need it on Day Five of Week Six from after breakfast time (about 9:00 a.m.) until the early evening (about 5:00 p.m.).
2. Take a fifteen- to thirty-minute silent prayer walk.
    a. Walk alone.
    b. Select a place where you are not likely to be disturbed, somewhere safe, quiet, and as pleasant as possible.
    c. As you walk, ask the Lord, "When today have I reacted when You would have preferred for me to be still? Why?"
3. What were the Lord's answers to your questions?

Journal

Record ideas, impressions, feelings, questions, and any insights you may have had during today's time.

Prayer

Pray for each member of your community.

Influence

DAY FIVE

Prayer

Dear Lord, teach me how to make myself available for You to lead others through me. Teach me what to say and when it is best for me to speak. Train me to serve You silently, to wait until Your Word commandeers my voice to speak. Amen.

Core Thought

> To lead as Jesus led we must be both common and extraordinary.

It has been said that success lies not so much in being well accomplished at doing extraordinary things but in accomplishing common things extraordinarily well. At first, these two characteristics, common and extraordinary, seem to be contradictory. However, this is not so with regard to leading with transformed influence. The key is knowing what it means to be common in an extraordinary way.

These days, being called common is not usually meant as a compliment. It is a put-down. It is said of someone or something to mean that he (or it) is less valuable for not being rare in quantity or quality. However, the leader who is common in the sense we as the authors mean is usually considered a rare and exceptional individual and is often highly valued by those whom he leads.

This idea that one must be common and extraordinary to lead as Jesus did means that for God to use a leader to spread His transforming influence, that leader must make herself available and accessible to the people whom God desires to transform. Influence cannot happen in isolation, so leaders must take extraordinary steps to make themselves available to those they lead. A leader must establish a habit of setting apart time in their schedule dedicated to being with those whom God wishes to influence. But simply being available to influence is not enough. To lead as Jesus led a leader must take extraordinary measures to ensure that God's transforming influence is accessible to those who will follow their leading.

Jesus is the perfect example of the leader who can influence different kinds of people by delivering God's transforming power in ways that make its truths easily accessible. Jesus always makes the way He influences someone match the way they can receive its truth. With a learned Pharisee, Jesus argues as a rabbi (John 3:1-21); with fishermen, Jesus speaks as a tradesman (John 21:1-12); with a grieving sister, Jesus weeps (John 11:35). To lead as Jesus led a leader must consider and devise the best means for communicating God's transforming influence to each of those whom God has brought within their sphere of influence.

Transformed influence comes from transformed leaders who make themselves commonly available and accessible in extraordinary ways to deliver God's transforming power to those within Christ's church and to those without Christ throughout the world.

Today's Exercises

Core Scripture: 1 Peter 2:9-12
Read aloud 1 Peter 2:9-12.
Recite this week's memory verse aloud five times.

> And the things you have heard me say in the presence of many witnesses entrust to reliable men who will also be qualified to teach others. (2 Timothy 2:2)

Meditate on today's passage.

Request to Be in His Presence

"Dear Lord, bring me into the context of Your world."

1. *Read it*—Remember: We read now only what is there, to hear once again, only what was spoken then. Read 2 Timothy 2:19-21 at least twice, out loud.

2. *Think it*—select a portion, a phrase within the reading, and mull it over in your mind, thinking about the context and setting, reimagining the event, putting yourself into the situation. As you meditate, use all five senses to re-create the context and the setting by building the images that are supplied within the passages.

3. *Pray it*—ask God to give you understanding into how the truths He has spoken in these Scriptures apply to you now. Ask, "What is it about me that I need to deal with? What is it about me that must change?"

    Respond to God by accepting and admitting whatever responsibility is implied by what He has shown. Write what it is that God has shown you, and what you must admit responsibility for having done (or not done).

4. *Live it*—ask God to reveal to you what He wants you to do about what you have admitted.

State what God has revealed that you must admit responsibility for doing.

State what particular action(s) you will take today to accomplish what God has revealed for you to do.

Doing the Discipline: Silence and Solitude
Practicing the Discipline of Solitude

1. Take a fifteen- to thirty-minute silent prayer walk.
   a. Walk alone.
   b. Select a place where you are not likely to be disturbed, somewhere safe, quiet, and as pleasant as possible.
   c. As you walk, ask the Lord, "When today have I reacted when You would have preferred for me to be still? Why?"
2. What was the Lord's answers to the question you asked each day during your silent prayer walk?
   Write the answers below.
   Day One:

   Day Two:

Day Three:

Day Four:

Day Five:

Journal

Record ideas, impressions, feelings, questions, and any insights you may have had during today's time.

Prayer

Pray for each member of your community.

Influence

DAY SIX

Community Meeting

In preparation for this week's meeting, you will have read and reflected upon each of the week's five Core Thoughts, recorded your thoughts and observations, and are ready to recite this week's memory verse to the group.

WEEK TWO

The Leadership Trap

DAY ONE

Prayer

Father, train into me a keen sense for detecting the presence of all kinds of traps by which the Devil intends to ensnare me. Lord, I ask today for Your wisdom because I lack it. Lead me out of the traps where my path has led me, save me from the traps that detour me from Your path. Amen.

Core Thought

> Most leaders in the church are caught in a trap
> set by the Devil, and rather than seeking their own
> deliverance, they have taken up the sport of trapping.

As a boy I arose early on Saturdays so I (Bill) could get my chores done in order to watch my favorite program, *The Three Stooges*. Even today I laugh out loud when I catch a few minutes of their slapstick antics. I remember Curly calling out in panic, "Moe, Larry, CHEESE." It would always be a moment of personal crisis for Curly, usually when he was about to lose control and hurt someone. So Moe and Larry would rush to get Curly some cheese; they would stuff it in his mouth and Curly would magically become calm. Cheese was what Curly needed, and once that need was met he would be fine until the next crisis. Cheese is what culture offers the spiritual leader to quiet our manic need for adulation and acceptance.

It seems that many leaders are just as frantic about needing their cheese as Curly. I know that I have been, and I couldn't feel good about life unless I was getting my ego needs met regularly. How many accolades was I getting about my messages, books, and leadership? Where was I invited to speak and by whom and before how many? This is all part of the cheese, the needs that must be met. It is the delectable morsel that is readily available and quick to satisfy, but it's a trap set for an animal that enters the cage to get its needs met and suddenly the door slams behind it and there it is, a prisoner. That trap is the prevailing pattern for church leadership.

We find ourselves trapped in a world that rewards numerical and financial success. This mind-set is just as real in the church world as any. We try to be successful by working to grow a church. If we grow a big one, then there is plenty of cheese. If not, we are trapped in the cage but without cheese. We read books and go to conferences where the big cheese leaders talk about their success. We return home and try out their methods and programs, and guess what? They don't work the same. Then we find ourselves trapped in this system where recognition is supreme. Oscar Wilde once said, "There are only two tragedies in life: one is not getting what one wants, and the other is getting it."

Those who are trapped in the American church system of rewards and punishments strive to do what works in order to build a career, climb the ecclesiastical ladder, and get the recognition and feedback needed to build a desired image. This does not mean it is evil to have a good career or any of the attributes above. What it does mean, however, is that many will fail by these standards and will be punished by a lack of rewards such as higher salaries, larger churches, and recognition among their peers. It is tragic when a person is trapped in a system in which he is moderately successful and largely unrewarded. As one sage put it, "There is nothing as sad as a man who is mediocre at what he loves." The church has told him or her by what it honors and ignores that he is average, mediocre, regular, not one of the elite.

It is a tragedy when someone is made to feel mediocre, and it is just as tragic that church culture behaves this way and that too many leaders go along with it. The other tragedy, however, is those who do succeed, because they are trapped in the same system that is temporarily working for them. They become addicted to the same superficial reward system that will eventually run out and leave them desperate.[1]

Today's Exercises

Core Scripture: 2 Timothy 2:22-26

Read aloud 2 Timothy 2:22-26.

Recite this week's memory verses aloud five times.

> And the Lord's servant must not quarrel; instead, he must be kind to everyone, able to teach, not resentful. Those who oppose him he must gently instruct, in the hope that God will grant them repentance leading them to a knowledge of the truth, and that they will come to their senses and escape from the trap of the devil, who has taken them captive to do his will. (2 Timothy 2:24-26)

Meditate on today's passage.

Request to Be in His Presence

"Dear Lord, bring me into the context of Your world."

1. *Read it*—Remember: We read now only what is there, to hear once again, only what was spoken then. Read John 3:1-2 at least twice, out loud.
2. *Think it*—select a portion, a phrase within the reading, and mull it over in your mind, thinking about the context and setting, reimagining the event, putting yourself into the situation. As you meditate, use all five senses to re-create the context and the setting by building the images that are supplied within the passages.

---

1. Bill Hull, *Choose the Life: Exploring a Faith that Embraces Discipleship* (Grand Rapids, MI: Baker, 2006), 181–182.

3. *Pray it*—ask God to give you understanding into how the truths He has spoken in these Scriptures apply to you now. Ask, "What is it about me that I need to deal with? What is it about me that must change?"

   Respond to God by accepting and admitting whatever responsibility is implied by what He has shown. Write what it is that God has shown you, and what you must admit responsibility for having done (or not done).

4. *Live it*—ask God to reveal to you what He wants you to do about what you have admitted.

State what God has revealed that you must admit responsibility for doing.

State what particular action(s) you will take today to accomplish what God has revealed for you to do.

Discovering the Discipline: Silence and Solitude

Last week, we said that the spiritual disciplines of solitude and silence are the primary starting point for a leader who wants to be transformed by God and lead others into the same experience. We also said that the two disciplines go hand in hand. Solitude uses silence, and silence, solitude.

Today, we will continue our discovery by understanding what the spiritual discipline of silence is and why it should be practiced.

As before, Dallas Willard gives us a very workable definition of the spiritual discipline of silence:

> Silence is a natural part of solitude and is its essential comple-
> tion. Most noise is human contact. Silence means to escape
> from sounds, noises, other than the gentle ones of nature. But
> it also means not talking, and the effects of not talking on
> our soul are different from those of simple quietness. Both
> dimensions of silence are crucial for the breaking of old habits
> and the formation of Christ's character in us. . . . Silence goes
> beyond solitude, and without it solitude has little effect. Henri
> Nouwen observes that "silence is the way to make solitude a
> reality. . . . In silence we close off our souls from 'sounds,'
> whether those sounds be noise, music, or words."[2]

Before we make our escape from the noise that surrounds us, it would be good for us to know in what ways it may be imprisoning us and what it does when we are its captive.

> Total silence is rare, and what we today call "quiet" usually
> only amounts to a little less noise. . . . Our households and
> offices are filled with the whirring, buzzing, murmuring, chat-
> tering, and whining of the multiple contraptions. . . . *Their
> noise comforts us* in some curious way. In fact, we find complete
> silence shocking because it leaves the impression that nothing
> is happening. In a go-go world such as ours, what could be
> worse than that! . . . But silence is frightening because it strips
> us as nothing else does, throwing us upon the stark realities of
> our life. It reminds us of death, which will cut us off from this
> world and leave only us and God. And in that quiet, what if
> there turns out to be very little to "just us and God"? Think

---

2. Hull, 163.

what it says about the inward emptiness of our lives if we must always turn on the tape player or radio to make sure something is happening around us. . . . Only silence will allow us life-transforming concentration upon God. It allows us to hear the gentle God whose only Son "shall not strive, nor cry; neither shall any man hear his voice above the street noise" (Matt. 12:19). It is this God who tells us that "in quietness and trust is your strength" (Isa. 30:15, NASB).

Sound always strikes deeply and disturbingly into our souls. So, for the sake of our souls, we must seek times to leave our television, radio, iPods, and telephones turned off. We should close off street noises as much as possible. We should try to find how quiet we can make our world by making whatever arrangements are necessary.

For instance, many have learned to rise for a time in the middle of the night—to break the night's sleep in half in order to experience such silence. In doing so, they find a rich silence that aids their prayer and study without imposing on others. And though it sounds impossible, meaningful progress into silence can be made without solitude, even within family life. And sharing this discipline with those you love may be exactly what is needed.[3]

Practicing the Discipline of Silence
Today, and for the remainder of the week:
1. Make your working environment as quiet as possible.
   a. Turn off all devices that create background sounds (TVs and radios).
   b. Don't use the entertainment system in your vehicle.
   c. Wear earplugs (when allowable and safe).
2. Take a fifteen- to thirty-minute silent prayer walk.

---

3. Hull, 163–164.

a. Walk alone.

b. Select a place where you are not likely to be disturbed, somewhere safe, quiet, and as pleasant as possible.

c. As you walk, ask the Lord, "What are the noises that I rely upon to make me feel comfortable, to tell me that I am safe, in control, important, and keep me from feeling lonely?"

3. What were the Lord's answers to your questions?

Journal

Record ideas, impressions, feelings, questions, and any insights you may have had during today's time.

Prayer

Pray for each member of your community.

The Leadership Trap

DAY TWO

Prayer

Dear Lord, help me to get a case of "get over it." Train me to believe and serve others as though it isn't all about me . . . because, after all, I really know it isn't. Train me to lead others by the example of my uncompromising commitment to accomplishing only Your will only Your way for only Your approval. Amen.

Core Thought

> The way out of the leadership trap is to commit ourselves to being irrelevant to what culture says is important.

Regardless of where you are on the American church food chain, you need to escape the tyranny of superficial goals and rewards. We have been told to always lead with our résumé—the sanitized and enhanced version of ourselves. For instance, my résumé or biographical sketch tells my life's mission, the books I have written, the positions I have held, and the dreams I hold dear. Historically it was common to include a statement such as, "and is in constant demand as a speaker and adviser." This makes me cringe, and thankfully it is on its way out. But for years it was an important part of résumé style, which I feel points to our need to be identified as important, relevant, wise, and with a lot to offer. This reflects the cultural need of many of us to have our importance reinforced.

Even successful leaders by contemporary standards can be just as miserable as those who are failing, because they have all their identity needs met but now realize how empty they are. So many thought there were rich rewards to be found in success measured in fame, recognition from peers, and the praise of the masses only to find it vacuous and unable to satisfy the hunger of the soul. But how does one escape?

What if my résumé read something like this:

Bill Hull has been in ministry for thirty-four years. It has been marked by several apparent successes recognized by thousands of readers, parishioners, and conferees. However, in his early fifties, Bill found himself hungry for something more satisfying. He had been living a life based on a false identity carved out of public opinion. He was conducting his pastoral life based on principles and formulas. His foundation for daily ministry was a competence developed through hard work and faithfulness. Then God decided to break Bill through a series of trials, rejection of his ministry, lack of measurable success, personal pain, and repentance. In desperation, Bill humbled himself before God not just in words but in practice by deciding to be irrelevant as Jesus was irrelevant and by daily deciding to follow Jesus and to lay aside the ways in which he used to measure success. Bill now has plenty of free time to tell his story of how irrelevant and unnecessary he really is.

Is there a better way, a different way of being that satisfies for the long term? Is there a way of living and following Jesus that will open a new door to a deeper and stronger life? I want to scream, "Yes, yes, yes!"

Henri Nouwen wrote, "I am deeply convinced that the Christian leader of the future is called to be completely irrelevant and to stand in this world with nothing to offer but his or her own vulnerable self."[4] This means to lead with your weakness.

To lead as Jesus led we must lead from the same quality of character that Jesus possessed. Doing so allowed Him to be unmoved by any feeling that He must remain relevant to the values of the culture of His day. It freed Him to accomplish God's will God's way.

Jesus' irrelevancy is the most relevant quality to others, for it is a humility that submits itself to loving and serving others and that is the most

---

4. Henri Nouwan, *In the Name of Jesus: Reflections on Christian Leadership* (New York: Crossroad, 1989), 17.

powerful force known to any of us. A choice to be irrelevant in the same way Jesus was irrelevant means to submit ourselves to His ways and means. It means becoming irrelevant to what our culture says is important.

Today's Exercises

Core Scripture: 2 Timothy 2:22-26

Read aloud 2 Timothy 2:22-26.

Recite this week's memory verses aloud five times.

> And the Lord's servant must not quarrel; instead, he must be kind to everyone, able to teach, not resentful. Those who oppose him he must gently instruct, in the hope that God will grant them repentance leading them to a knowledge of the truth, and that they will come to their senses and escape from the trap of the devil, who has taken them captive to do his will. (2 Timothy 2:24-26)

Meditate on today's passage.

Request to Be in His Presence

"Dear Lord, bring me into the context of Your world."

1. **Read it**—Remember: We read now only what is there, to hear once again, only what was spoken then. Read John 3:3-5 at least twice, out loud.
2. **Think it**—select a portion, a phrase within the reading, and mull it over in your mind, thinking about the context and setting, reimagining the event, putting yourself into the situation. As you meditate, use all five senses to re-create the context and the setting by building the images that are supplied within the passages.
3. **Pray it**—ask God to give you understanding into how the truths He has spoken in these Scriptures apply to you now. Ask, "What is it about me that I need to deal with? What is it about me that must change?"

Respond to God by accepting and admitting whatever responsibility is implied by what He has shown. Write what it is that God has shown you, and what you must admit responsibility for having done (or not done).

4. *Live it*—ask God to reveal to you what He wants you to do about what you have admitted.

State what God has revealed that you must admit responsibility for doing.

State what particular action(s) you will take today to accomplish what God has revealed for you to do.

Doing the Discipline: Silence and Solitude
Practicing the Discipline of Silence
Today:

1. Make your working environment as quiet as possible.
   a. Turn off all devices that create background sounds (TVs and radios).
   b. Don't use the entertainment system in your vehicle.
   c. Wear earplugs (when allowable and safe).
2. Take a fifteen- to thirty-minute silent prayer walk.
   a. Walk alone.

b. Select a place where you are not likely to be disturbed, somewhere safe, quiet, and as pleasant as possible.

c. As you walk, ask the Lord, "What are the noises that I rely upon to make me feel comfortable, to tell me that I am safe, in control, important, and keep me from feeling lonely?"

3. What were the Lord's answers to your questions?

Journal

Record ideas, impressions, feelings, questions, and any insights you may have had during today's time.

Prayer

Pray for each member of your community.

The Leadership Trap

DAY THREE

Prayer

Dear Lord, teach me not to pay attention to the groaning of my inse-
curities when they tell me that I had better make something happen
pretty soon if I want to keep folks thinking I'm successful. And when
I do accomplish something well, train me to ignore my ego when it
begins to demand that I do something about how others are failing to
give me the recognition I surely deserve. Lord, help free me from the
tyranny of my need for the approval of others. Amen.

Core Thought

> To escape the trap, we must become
> unnecessary to what we ourselves feel is essential.

I (Bill) have never been able to escape the feeling that I, as a pastor, am
responsible for my church. It occurred to me one day that I was not pastor-
ing the church as much as I was running the church. There are a number
of reasons for believing this. First, when a pastor resigns, the church goes
into a holding pattern while they search for a new pastor. Second, people
expect leadership, and we attend seminars and read books on how to do it.
If we do not lead, we are considered derelict, not gifted or blessed of God.
Third, people measure the church's success by the pastor's performance
and determine each week how things are going by the sermon.

It is for these reasons and more that we pastors, and others who
lead in church ministry, feel indispensable and important to the work.
After all, if I don't run this place, we might ask, who will? Our response

should not be to become passive. Instead we need to consider how we lead and how we invest our time. If a ministry in the church falls apart because we don't run it in the traditional sense, it proves that we were not building the ministry on the right foundation. We should ask ourselves what life would be like if we only did the things Scripture describes as essential for spiritual development.

Eugene Peterson was pastor of a Presbyterian church for many years. At one point he felt very strongly that he was engaging in non-pastoral activities that were expected of him but that he also felt were important in order to retain control. He made a decision to stop attending all committee meetings except for the elders' meeting. Some time later he dropped by a committee meeting and one of the members asked, "What are you doing here? Don't you trust us?" At that Peterson left and never returned because he realized he was unnecessary.

What would it be like if we could influence others through our character and teaching? What would it be like if who we are was so powerful that we didn't need organizational infrastructure to make things happen?[5]

Today's Exercises

Core Scripture: 2 Timothy 2:22-26
Read aloud 2 Timothy 2:22-26.
Recite this week's memory verses aloud five times.

> And the Lord's servant must not quarrel; instead, he must be kind to everyone, able to teach, not resentful. Those who oppose him he must gently instruct, in the hope that God will grant them repentance leading them to a knowledge of the truth, and that they will come to their senses and escape from the trap of the devil, who has taken them captive to do his will. (2 Timothy 2:24-26)

Meditate on today's passage.

---

5. Hull, *Choose the Life*, 187–188.

Request to Be in His Presence

"Dear Lord, bring me into the context of Your world."

1. *Read it*—Remember: We read now only what is there, to hear once again, only what was spoken then. Read John 3:6-8 at least twice, out loud.
2. *Think it*—select a portion, a phrase within the reading, and mull it over in your mind, thinking about the context and setting, reimagining the event, putting yourself into the situation. As you meditate, use all five senses to re-create the context and the setting by building the images that are supplied within the passages.
3. *Pray it*—ask God to give you understanding into how the truths He has spoken in these Scriptures apply to you now. Ask, "What is it about me that I need to deal with? What is it about me that must change?"

   Respond to God by accepting and admitting whatever responsibility is implied by what He has shown. Write what it is that God has shown you, and what you must admit responsibility for having done (or not done).
4. *Live it*—ask God to reveal to you what He wants you to do about what you have admitted.

State what God has revealed that you must admit responsibility for doing.

State what particular action(s) you will take today to accomplish what God has revealed for you to do.

Doing the Discipline: Silence and Solitude

Practicing the Discipline of Silence

Today:

1. Make your working environment as quiet as possible.
   a. Turn off all devices that create background sounds (TVs and radios).
   b. Don't use the entertainment system in your vehicle.
   c. Wear earplugs (when allowable and safe).
2. Take a fifteen- to thirty-minute silent prayer walk.
   a. Walk alone.
   b. Select a place where you are not likely to be disturbed, somewhere safe, quiet, and as pleasant as possible.
   c. As you walk, ask the Lord, "What are the noises that I rely upon to make me feel comfortable, to tell me that I am safe, in control, important, and keep me from feeling lonely?"
3. What were the Lord's answers to your questions?

Journal

Record ideas, impressions, feelings, questions, and any insights you may have had during today's time.

Prayer

Pray for each member of your community.

The Leadership Trap

DAY FOUR

Prayer

Dear Father, help me to care so little about how much others are valuing me that others will value You for how much I am caring for others. Amen.

Core Thought

> To escape the trap we must become unnecessary to what people insist we do for them.

[Our] culture tells us that people who are leaders in the Church are to be nice people who open the Little League season with a prayer or say a benediction at the dedication of a new building site. Culture allows us to pepper people's lives with a little moral truth now and then to get them through the hard times. Most of all culture wants those who minister to be chaplains, to marry, bury, and perform the duties of our society. Whenever we accept this as our role, we are finished as spiritual leaders.

Jesus said, "I have come to bring fire on the earth" (Luke 12:49). Our radical nature is expressed in our stubborn insistence that we follow the humility and submission of Jesus in His agenda and ways of touching others.[6]

---

6. Hull, *Choose the Life*, 186–187.

There is not much interest in humility and submission or in becoming irrelevant and unnecessary:

> Have you read a book on how to do that lately? We all give it the polite nod, but how many of us are ready to choose to follow Jesus in this? We cannot truly follow Jesus without committing to His commitment to humility and submission, to being irrelevant and unnecessary to what society (yes, even the religious society) values.[7]

To lead as Jesus led we must stop trying to obtain affirmation from the people we serve for satisfying their culturally formed appetites. The more they insist that we do so, the more we must resist. And the more silent their approval grows, the louder we must denounce our need for it.

Today's Exercises
Core Scripture: 2 Timothy 2:22-26
Read aloud 2 Timothy 2:22-26.
Recite this week's memory verses aloud five times.

> And the Lord's servant must not quarrel; instead, he must be kind to everyone, able to teach, not resentful. Those who oppose him he must gently instruct, in the hope that God will grant them repentance leading them to a knowledge of the truth, and that they will come to their senses and escape from the trap of the devil, who has taken them captive to do his will. (2 Timothy 2:24-26)

Meditate on today's passage.

Request to Be in His Presence
"Dear Lord, bring me into the context of Your world."

---

7. Hull, *Choose the Life*, 188.

1. ***Read it***—Remember: We read now only what is there, to hear once again, only what was spoken then. Read John 3:9-12 at least twice, out loud.

2. ***Think it***—select a portion, a phrase within the reading, and mull it over in your mind, thinking about the context and setting, reimagining the event, putting yourself into the situation. As you meditate, use all five senses to re-create the context and the setting by building the images that are supplied within the passages.

3. ***Pray it***—ask God to give you understanding into how the truths He has spoken in these Scriptures apply to you now. Ask, "What is it about me that I need to deal with? What is it about me that must change?"

   Respond to God by accepting and admitting whatever responsibility is implied by what He has shown. Write what it is that God has shown you, and what you must admit responsibility for having done (or not done).

4. ***Live it***—ask God to reveal to you what He wants you to do about what you have admitted.

State what God has revealed that you must admit responsibility for doing.

State what particular action(s) you will take today to accomplish what God has revealed for you to do.

Doing the Discipline: Silence and Solitude

Practicing the Discipline of Silence

Today:

1. Make your working environment as quiet as possible.
    a. Turn off all devices that create background sounds (TVs and radios).
    b. Don't use the entertainment system in your vehicle.
    c. Wear earplugs (when allowable and safe).
2. Take a fifteen- to thirty-minute silent prayer walk.
    a. Walk alone.
    b. Select a place where you are not likely to be disturbed, somewhere safe, quiet, and as pleasant as possible.
    c. As you walk, ask the Lord, "What are the noises that I rely upon to make me feel comfortable, to tell me that I am safe, in control, important, and keep me from feeling lonely?"
3. What were the Lord's answers to your questions?

Journal

Record ideas, impressions, feelings, questions, and any insights you may have had during today's time.

Prayer

Pray for each member of your community.

The Leadership Trap

DAY FIVE

Prayer

Dear Lord, teach me a new way to understand success and what it means to be successful. Teach me Your way. Help me to see what it will look like when I am being successful as You see it. Amen.

Core Thought

> To lead as Jesus led we must train to dislodge the world's images of success from our understanding and replace them with the transforming and victorious image of the crucified and risen Savior.

The world's and the American church's images of success have become so ingrained in our consciousness and so form the bulk of our understanding that there is barely any room remaining for the truth to wedge itself into. But as long as even the tiniest space remains, the wrecking ball of truth will break open even the strongest barrier and allow the light to shine in upon its rightful domain.

Let us be clear about one thing: to lead as Jesus led requires that we lead with the same quality of character that Jesus has, and that character is formed in us beginning with the renewing of our minds (Romans 12:2). To lead as Jesus led we must train to dislodge the world's images of success from our understanding (from our minds) and replace them with the transforming and victorious image of the crucified and risen Savior. Remember, it is first the battle to renew the mind. The weapons we will use to dislodge the world's images and its notions of success are the cross of Christ and the empty tomb.

We must intentionally reintroduce to our minds in prayer and meditation, by studying God's Word, by serving devotedly in Jesus' name, in sharing the Lord's Supper, and by witnessing believers being baptized, this truth: the greatest success that will ever be achieved was accomplished through humility and submission. It is the humiliation of the cross that brought about the ultimate success, and an empty tomb was the sign that the greatest accomplishment had been achieved. The cross declares that the world's ideas of success are the empty lies of the Devil, and it casts them out. The empty tomb heralds the fullness of Christ's victory and ushers in His resurrection power.

For us to lead as Jesus led, the image of the cross of Christ and the truth of Christ's resurrection must so form and fill our understanding that anything which passes before our mind's consciousness becomes relevant only insofar as it bears witness to their truth and brings honor to Christ.

Today's Exercises
Core Scripture: 2 Timothy 2:22-26
Read aloud 2 Timothy 2:22-26.
Recite this week's memory verses aloud five times.

> And the Lord's servant must not quarrel; instead, he must be kind to everyone, able to teach, not resentful. Those who oppose him he must gently instruct, in the hope that God will grant them repentance leading them to a knowledge of the truth, and that they will come to their senses and escape from the trap of the devil, who has taken them captive to do his will. (2 Timothy 2:24-26)

Meditate on today's passage.

Request to Be in His Presence
"Dear Lord, bring me into the context of Your world."

1. *Read it*—Remember: We read now only what is there, to hear once again, only what was spoken then. Read John 3:13-15 at least twice, out loud.

2. *Think it*—select a portion, a phrase within the reading, and mull it over in your mind, thinking about the context and setting, reimagining the event, putting yourself into the situation. As you meditate, use all five senses to re-create the context and the setting by building the images that are supplied within the passages.

3. *Pray it*—ask God to give you understanding into how the truths He has spoken in these Scriptures apply to you now. Ask, "What is it about me that I need to deal with? What is it about me that must change?"

   Respond to God by accepting and admitting whatever responsibility is implied by what He has shown. Write what it is that God has shown you, and what you must admit responsibility for having done (or not done).

4. *Live it*—ask God to reveal to you what He wants you to do about what you have admitted.

State what God has revealed that you must admit responsibility for doing.

State what particular action(s) you will take today to accomplish what God has revealed for you to do.

Doing the Discipline: Silence and Solitude

Practicing the Discipline of Silence

Today:

1. Make your working environment as quiet as possible.
   a. Turn off all devices that create background sounds (TVs and radios).
   b. Don't use the entertainment system in your vehicle.
   c. Wear earplugs (when allowable and safe).
2. Take a fifteen- to thirty-minute silent prayer walk.
   a. Walk alone.
   b. Select a place where you are not likely to be disturbed, somewhere safe, quiet, and as pleasant as possible.
   c. As you walk, ask the Lord, "What are the noises that I rely upon to make me feel comfortable, to tell me that I am safe, in control, important, and keep me from feeling lonely?"
3. What was the Lord's answers to the question you asked each day during your silent prayer walk?
   Write the answers below.
   Day One:

   Day Two:

   Day Three:

Day Four:

Day Five:

Journal

Record ideas, impressions, feelings, questions, and any insights you may have had during today's time.

Prayer

Pray for each member of your community.

The Leadership Trap

DAY SIX

Community Meeting

In preparation for this week's meeting, you will have read and reflected upon each of the week's five Core Thoughts, recorded your thoughts and observations, and are ready to recite this week's memory verses to the group.

WEEK THREE

Give Up the Gods

DAY ONE

Prayer

Dear Lord, I'm sorry for being more concerned about accomplishing what my religious culture compels me to do than about accomplishing what You have commanded me to do. Please help me to kick my addiction to pleasing the gods of my religious culture. Amen.

Core Thought

> Influencing others from the purity of our character requires that we kick our addiction to the gods of our religious culture.

Getting off the gods of our religious culture to which we are addicted is like going through detox. Their allure is strong enough it might require beginning with a complete separation from the conditions in which we live. That could be followed by a halfway house and practicing the new life with a strong support system.

My oldest son was caught up in the destructive nature of our culture. He was headed down the wrong road and was getting his needs for significance met in the wrong places. We sent him to a school for hard-to-parent teens for a year in the Dominican Republic. He didn't watch television or listen to the music of our culture; he lived without the noise and distraction. The total separation from his culture gave him a chance to get it all out of his system.

Please don't misunderstand me; we are not like confused teens living destructive lives. We are leaders who love and desire to follow Jesus but are addicted to a religious culture that is not working for many of us.[1]

So what are the gods that must go? They are the gods of competition, attendance, progress, and competence.

For the remainder of the week, we will discuss how these gods and their myths affect those who lead in Christ's churches, what must be done to eradicate their influence, and how leaders can exercise transformed influence in their churches and in the world.

Today's Exercises

Core Scripture: 2 Timothy 3:1-17

Read aloud 2 Timothy 3:1-17.

Recite this week's memory verses aloud five times.

> But as for you, continue in what you have learned and have become convinced of, because you know those from whom you learned it, and how from infancy you have known the holy Scriptures, which are able to make you wise for salvation through faith in Christ Jesus. (2 Timothy 3:14-15)

Meditate on today's passage.

Request to Be in His Presence

"Dear Lord, bring me into the context of Your world."

1. *Read it*—Remember: We read now only what is there, to hear once again, only what was spoken then. Read John 3:22-26 at least twice, out loud.

2. *Think it*—select a portion, a phrase within the reading, and mull it over in your mind, thinking about the context and setting,

---

1. Bill Hull, *Choose the Life: Exploring a Faith that Embraces Discipleship* (Grand Rapids, MI: Baker, 2006), 189.

reimagining the event, putting yourself into the situation. As you meditate, use all five senses to re-create the context and the setting by building the images that are supplied within the passages.

3. *Pray it*—ask God to give you understanding into how the truths He has spoken in these Scriptures apply to you now. Ask, "What is it about me that I need to deal with? What is it about me that must change?"

    Respond to God by accepting and admitting whatever responsibility is implied by what He has shown. Write what it is that God has shown you, and what you must admit responsibility for having done (or not done).

4. *Live it*—ask God to reveal to you what He wants you to do about what you have admitted.

State what God has revealed that you must admit responsibility for doing.

State what particular action(s) you will take today to accomplish what God has revealed for you to do.

Discovering the Discipline: Silence and Solitude

Last week, we discussed the first dimension of the spiritual discipline of silence, removing ourselves from the comfort of the company of many sounds. Today, we will discuss the second dimension, removing ourselves from the comfort of the company of our own speaking. Both dimensions of silence are crucial for the breaking of old habits and the formation of Christ's character in us.

Dallas Willard continues by helping us to understand this dimension of silence:

> We must also practice the silence of not speaking. James, in his Epistle, tells us that those who seem religious but are unable to bridle their tongues are self-deceived and have a religion that amounts to little (James 1:26). He states that those who do no harm by what they say are perfect and able to direct their whole bodies to do what is right (James 3:2).
>
> Practice in not speaking can at least give us enough control over what we say that our tongues do not "go off" automatically. This discipline provides us with a certain inner distance that gives us time to consider our words fully and the presence of mind to control what we say and when we say it. . . . Such practice also helps us to listen and to observe, to pay attention to people. How rarely are we ever truly listened to, and how deep is our need to be heard. I wonder how much wrath in human life is a result of not being heard. James says, "Let every man be swift to hear, slow to speak, slow to wrath" (1:19). Yet when the tongue is moving rapidly, it seems wrath will usually be found following it.
>
> Why do we insist on talking as much as we do? We run off at the mouth because we are inwardly uneasy about what others think of us. Eberhard Arnold observes: "People who love one another can be silent together." But when we're with those we feel less than secure with, we use words to "adjust" our appearance and elicit their approval. Otherwise, we fear our virtues might not receive adequate appreciation and our shortcomings might not be properly "understood." In not speaking, we resign how we appear (dare we say, how we are?) to God. And that is hard. Why should we worry about others'

opinions of us when God is for us and Jesus Christ is on his right hand pleading our interests (Rom. 8:31-34)? But we do.[2]

How few of us live with quiet, inner confidence, and yet how many of us desire it. Inward quiet is a great grace we can receive as we practice not talking. And when we have it, we may be able to help others who need it. After we know that confidence, we may, when others come fishing for reassurance and approval, send them to fish in deeper waters for their own inner quiet.

Doing the Discipline: Silence and Solitude
Practicing the Discipline of Silence
Today, and for remainder of the week:

1. Make your conversation full of meaning but not full of words.
   a. Allow others to speak twice as much as you by listening to them twice as much as you speak.
   b. Do not interrupt others when they are speaking.
   c. Do not think about the next thing you want to say when someone is speaking to you.
   d. Pause for two seconds to think about what you are going to say before you make any reply.
2. Take a fifteen- to thirty-minute silent prayer walk.
   a. Walk alone.
   b. Select a place where you are not likely to be disturbed, somewhere safe, quiet, and as pleasant as possible.
   c. As you walk, ask the Lord, "When have I spoken today when You would have preferred for me to be silent? Why then?"
3. What were the Lord's answers to your questions?

---

2. Dallas Willard, *The Spirit of the Disciplines* (San Francisco: Harper & Row, 1992), 160–165.

Journal

Record ideas, impressions, feelings, questions, and any insights you may have had during today's time.

Prayer

Pray for each member of your community.

Give Up the Gods

DAY TWO

Prayer

Dear Lord, I confess that there were many times when my motivation for serving You was more about working hard to show others that I can do it better than others can. Well, really it was to prove to everyone that I am better than others. Yes, Lord, I do know better. Please train me to lead Your way. Lord, I'm so tired. Amen.

Core Thought

> To exercise transformed influence, leaders must forsake the god of competition and forget the practice of nose-counting.

People who make up the American church culture want leaders who are winners. They expect a new leader to ride in on a white charger to save the day and take their church to the next level. They are ready for their church to make its mark, to become a large regional church, and then experience God's blessing. In other words, without knowing or articulating it, they have asked their new leaders to lead them into the world of religious competition. They want a leader in the same way the Israelites wanted a king. They want a winner.

Our culture is drenched with the competitive spirit. It started for me (Bill) in Little League at age eight. I wanted to excel, and my popularity and self-worth were based on how I performed on the field. This followed me through my formative years and my athletic career and then went along for the ride into the pastoral life. Like most young pastors, my goals were scripturally based but driven by a personal need to succeed. This can cause our primary motivation to be competitive because we have been living in a false system. So instead of compassion being the earmark of our lives, we are caught up in a competition with other leaders to increase our influence (our market share) and thus our ministry cachet.

As a new leader, you enter into the competitive world of what is hottest—the most exciting and most productive. If you don't believe this is paramount, watch what happens when people start streaming out the door to the hottest new thing. Do you feel the pressure? Of course you do. Do you feel like you are failing? Yes. Do you have an identity crisis and wonder where God's blessing has gone? You bet. Do people start to question your leadership? They do, and if you don't seem as panicked as they are, then you don't care, you're not open, you're not growing, and you've gone to seed. You are not successful. You are not a winner!

Without a doubt, the single most important measure of success in our religious culture is attendance. We can deny it, but there is far too much evidence that this is the case. For example, we honor and extol the largest churches. Their pastors become an elite priesthood to whom others look for guidance. This belief system is crippling to the needed focus on what is required to fulfill the Great Commission.

I do not believe that pastors of large churches or the large churches themselves are the problem. What I am against is the belief that they are the standard by which we measure success. After all, their methods are at work in less than 3 percent of churches, appeal to motives that are less than healthy, are less successful in other sized churches, are highly dependent on the personal charisma of its public leadership for their success, and have reversed the flow that Scripture describes. The original churches met in homes and were kingdom outposts that stayed close to those who needed the gospel. The impulse to penetrate our world should be at least equal to the desire to gather for meetings. Consider Elton Trueblood's comments about our worship of church attendance:

> If Christianity is primarily a matter of attendance at a performance, it is not different in kind from a host of other

experiences. Though membership may include attendance at performances of a certain character, such attendance is not the primary meaning of the Christian effort at all. The fact that this is not generally understood is one of the chief evidences of the spiritual erosion which distresses us.[3]

The focus of the church is to gather in order to inspire, encourage, comfort, train, and mobilize the members to penetrate their world. The kingdom is to grow naturally through families and other networks. The focus is the church in the world more than the church gathered for a meeting. The overemphasis on a "worship service" is not only a misunderstanding of worship itself but is a tyranny in which many feel trapped.

One way to give up the god of attendance is to replace it with a different goal. Dallas Willard says it well: "We must flatly say that one of the greatest contemporary barriers to meaningful spiritual formation into Christlikeness is overconfidence in the spiritual efficacy of 'regular church services.' . . . Though they are vital, they are not enough. It is that simple."[4]

When our goal changes from recognition from others to the transformation of others, it is easy to put attendance in its place. If I am committed to humility and submission, then being irrelevant and unnecessary to the gods of my culture is easy. My commitment and reward as a leader is enrolling members into life and being a part of their transformation. That way every single leader can make it, succeed, and live out God's dream for him or her through who she is. Then attendance at meetings takes its place as one of the possible fruits of the work but not the ultimate proof of our talent and importance to God.

3. Elton Trueblood, *The Company of the Committed* (New York: Harper and Row, 1961), 20.

4. Dallas Willard, *Renovation of the Heart* (Colorado Springs, CO: NavPress, 2002), 250.

Today's Exercises

Core Scripture: 2 Timothy 3:1-17

Read aloud 2 Timothy 3:1-17.

Recite this week's memory verses aloud five times.

> But as for you, continue in what you have learned and have
> become convinced of, because you know those from whom
> you learned it, and how from infancy you have known the
> holy Scriptures, which are able to make you wise for salvation
> through faith in Christ Jesus. (2 Timothy 3:14-15)

Meditate on today's passage.

Request to Be in His Presence

   "Dear Lord, bring me into the context of Your world."

1. ***Read it***—Remember: We read now only what is there, to hear
   once again, only what was spoken then. Read John 3:27-28 at
   least twice, out loud.
2. ***Think it***—select a portion, a phrase within the reading, and mull
   it over in your mind, thinking about the context and setting,
   reimagining the event, putting yourself into the situation. As you
   meditate, use all five senses to re-create the context and the setting
   by building the images that are supplied within the passages.
3. ***Pray it***—ask God to give you understanding into how the truths
   He has spoken in these Scriptures apply to you now. Ask, "What
   is it about me that I need to deal with? What is it about me that
   must change?"
       Respond to God by accepting and admitting whatever
   responsibility is implied by what He has shown. Write what it is
   that God has shown you, and what you must admit responsibility
   for having done (or not done).
4. ***Live it***—ask God to reveal to you what He wants you to do
   about what you have admitted.

State what God has revealed that you must admit responsibility for doing.

State what particular action(s) you will take today to accomplish what God has revealed for you to do.

Doing the Discipline: Silence and Solitude
Practicing the Discipline of Silence
Today,
1. Make your conversation full of meaning but not full of words.
   a. Allow others to speak twice as much as you, by listening to them twice as much as you speak.
   b. Do not interrupt others when they are speaking.
   c. Do not think about the next thing you want to say when someone is speaking to you.
   d. Pause for two seconds, to think about what you are going to say before you make any reply.
2. Take a fifteen- to thirty-minute silent prayer walk.
   a. Walk alone.
   b. Select a place where you are not likely to be disturbed, somewhere safe, quiet, and as pleasant as possible.
   c. As you walk, ask the Lord, "When have I spoken today when You would have preferred for me to be silent? Why then?"

3. What were the Lord's answers to your questions?

Journal

Record ideas, impressions, feelings, questions, and any insights you may have had during today's time.

Prayer

Pray for each member of your community.

Give Up the Gods

DAY THREE

Prayer

Dear Lord, sometimes I dread doing what You have called me to do. I work hard so that I can be an example to the people I lead. Often, though, I don't see a lot of fruit resulting from all my hard work. I feel like I'm on some kind of ministry treadmill. I'm getting quite a work-out, and I'm tired, but I'm not convinced that it's getting me further toward my goals. If I'm not thinking about this the right way, Lord, then I need You to get me back on track. Amen.

Core Thought

> To exercise transformed influence, leaders must renounce the god of progress and reject its myth of lies.

"If you're not goin', you're not growin', and if you're not bigger than you were before, you're not growin', if you're not growin', then you're dyin'. And if you're dyin', get out of the way!" This is the call to worship of the god of progress. This manic need to increase and make things happen is at epidemic levels. The original American dream was freedom, liberty, and justice for all. Having these allowed us to engage in the "pursuit of happiness." After these were secured, the pursuit of happiness morphed into a scramble to accumulate wealth, and the American dream morphed into a materialistic dream. Now what people generally mean by the American dream is that your children will live better than you did, that each subsequent generation will be richer, smarter, healthier, and happier.

The American church has been baptized by immersion in the American dream, and many of its leaders have stayed under a bit too long and become saturated in its philosophy. This means that we expect the church and its ministries to grow and improve their programs every year. The unforgivable sin is for a church ministry to have a bad year. This is the myth of progress that was challenged by the late Christopher Lasch in *The True and Only Heaven*.

> How does it happen that serious people continue to believe in progress, in the face of massive evidence that might have been expected to refute the idea of progress once and for all? . . . Insatiable desire, formerly condemned as a source of frustration, unhappiness, and spiritual inability, came to be seen as a powerful stimulus to economic development. Instead of disparaging the tendency to want more than we need, liberals like Adam Smith argued that needs varied from one society to another, that civilized men needed more than savages to make them comfortable.[5]

The lie at the root of the myth of progress is that having more is always best no matter how it is obtained. It says that the quantity of something is always more important than the quality and that having the goods is more important than being good. The liar behind the myth of progress is the god of progress, Satan.

The Devil, dressed up as the god of progress, is simply retelling us now the original lies he told to man in the Garden of Eden, that God cannot be trusted, there is more to be possessed, it is now yours for the taking, and doing so is a good thing (Genesis 3:4-6). But doing so produced the only thing that comes from disobedience to God, not progress, but regress. Man did not progress toward being like God. He immediately began to retreat away from God (Genesis 3:8). The god of progress has been a liar from the beginning, as has been his myth of

---

5. Christopher Lasch, *The True and Only Heaven* (New York: Norton & Co., 1991), 13.

progress (John 8:44). One need only to look at the "progress" this myth has produced to know it is a lie: death from wars, death from starvation, death from totalitarian regimes, human slavery, animal cruelty, environmental devastation. The list goes on. The myth of progress has had only a deformational influence upon mankind.

To exercise transformed influence, leaders must renounce the god of progress and reject its myth of lies. This is done by embracing Jesus' way, the way of humility and submission. It is accomplished by living according to the beatific life Jesus commanded. Doing so trains us to "seek . . . first the kingdom of God, and his righteousness" (Matthew 6:33, KJV). By training in this way we will witness the truth of Jesus' promise that we can ask for anything in His name and the Father will surely give it to us (John 15:14-16).

Today's Exercises
Core Scripture: 2 Timothy 3:1-17
Read aloud 2 Timothy 3:1-17.
Recite this week's memory verses aloud five times.

> But as for you, continue in what you have learned and have become convinced of, because you know those from whom you learned it, and how from infancy you have known the holy Scriptures, which are able to make you wise for salvation through faith in Christ Jesus. (2 Timothy 3:14-15)

Meditate on today's passage.

Request to Be in His Presence
"Dear Lord, bring me into the context of Your world."

1. *Read it*—Remember: We read now only what is there, to hear once again, only what was spoken then. Read John 3:29 at least twice, out loud.
2. *Think it*—select a portion, a phrase within the reading, and mull

it over in your mind, thinking about the context and setting, reimagining the event, putting yourself into the situation. As you meditate, use all five senses to re-create the context and the setting by building the images that are supplied within the passages.

3. ***Pray it***—ask God to give you understanding into how the truths He has spoken in these Scriptures apply to you now. Ask, "What is it about me that I need to deal with? What is it about me that must change?"

    Respond to God by accepting and admitting whatever responsibility is implied by what He has shown. Write what it is that God has shown you, and what you must admit responsibility for having done (or not done).

4. ***Live it***—ask God to reveal to you what He wants you to do about what you have admitted.

State what God has revealed that you must admit responsibility for doing.

State what particular action(s) you will take today to accomplish what God has revealed for you to do.

Doing the Discipline: Silence and Solitude

Practicing the Discipline of Silence

Today:

1. Make your conversation full of meaning but not full of words.
   a. Allow others to speak twice as much as you, by listening to them twice as much as you speak.
   b. Do not interrupt others when they are speaking.
   c. Do not think about the next thing you want to say when someone is speaking to you.
   d. Pause for two seconds to think about what you are going to say before you make any reply.
2. Take a fifteen- to thirty-minute silent prayer walk.
   a. Walk alone.
   b. Select a place where you are not likely to be disturbed, somewhere safe, quiet, and as pleasant as possible.
   c. As you walk, ask the Lord, "When have I spoken today when You would have preferred for me to be silent? Why then?"
3. What were the Lord's answers to your questions?

Journal

Record ideas, impressions, feelings, questions, and any insights you may have had during today's time.

Prayer

Pray for each member of your community.

Give Up the Gods

DAY FOUR

Prayer

Dear Lord, a lot of things get done well because I do them. Is it so wrong for me to think that I am a good leader because I am gifted and can do so many things well? Isn't that why You give talents to people, so that they will be successful? A little help here, Lord? I must be missing something. Amen.

Core Thought

> To exercise transformed influence, leaders must denounce the god of competence and deny its myth of lies.

Part of the *esprit de corps* of successful leaders is that they have the right stuff. There is a feeling when leaders gather: We can relax now because we made the club. We are the elite who know how to make things grow; we make things happen. It is true that such a gathering is often one of very talented people, but it is also a cadre of myth-mongers perpetuating the lie that lives in the myth of competence.

The myth of competence is the idea that we will outgrow our weaknesses, difficult sins, fears, and disappointments. We will reach a place of spiritual competence where we have it together. It's a myth because that time never comes; in fact, our dependence on God grows as we become more like Jesus.

The god of competence proclaims that personal talent, charisma, intellectual prowess, and skill acquired through experience are all that is necessary to ensure a leader's success. And that a leader who has these things is rightfully recognized as having the right stuff.

In today's world, competency is the currency through which a leader purchases the influence necessary to advance his agenda. In the kingdom of this world, competency is king. But in Christ's kingdom this is not so.

For leaders in Christian ministry, personal competence is only a handmaiden of godly character. Our skill sets are meant to enhance our ability to serve others as we lead them. They are tools that our character calls upon when we lead. They are tools for doing work, not signage meant to advertise the value of our influence. Though a leader's competency may seem to reign supreme in the kingdom of this world, it certainly does not in Christ's kingdom. Understanding this is vital because we lead out of our character. Our character is our influence. It is only by our character that we have the power to affect any significant influence to change another's thoughts and actions.

Competence is a barrier; it makes people who see themselves as less competent feel that you don't understand them, and therefore, you cannot help them. My image of competence came through much stronger than my need of God's help, and it became my greatest barrier to connecting with others. My wife, Jane, has told me that the reason I tick some people off is that I make work look easy. When God broke me, He gave me words to express that brokenness in a way that got through to those around me. Then the real power of ministry came into my life, my preaching, and my personal interaction. They could see me as one of them—a fellow believer struggling daily to live out the life that Christ lived.

Our culture accepts the god of competence who says that pain and suffering is failure, that someone who struggles with fear and rejection is not walking with God. If they have these problems, then something has gone wrong—they made a mistake, they didn't listen, or they didn't read the right books.

Those who accept the god of competence never stop to remember that Jesus struggled. He was rejected; He failed in some of His work; He was considered a zealous idiot by many. What a glorious day when

I realized that Paul's wonderful words of honoring weakness were talking about me:

> And He [the Lord] said to me, "My grace is sufficient for you, for My strength is made perfect in weakness." Therefore most gladly I will rather boast in my infirmities, that the power of Christ may rest upon me. Therefore I take pleasure in infirmities, in reproaches, in needs, in persecutions, in distresses, for Christ's sake. For when I am weak, then I am strong. (2 Corinthians 12:9-10, NKJV)

Your competency may gain you attention, but only godly character can sustain the transforming influence necessary to lead others. Competence can take you far, but it won't take you and those who you lead where God has planned for you to go.

What can be done with competence alone is puny and meager compared to a life that is lived out of the character of Christ in us.

Today's Exercises

Core Scripture: 2 Timothy 3:1-17
Read aloud 2 Timothy 3:1-17.
Recite this week's memory verses aloud five times.

> But as for you, continue in what you have learned and have become convinced of, because you know those from whom you learned it, and how from infancy you have known the holy Scriptures, which are able to make you wise for salvation through faith in Christ Jesus. (2 Timothy 3:14-15)

Meditate on today's passage.

Request to Be in His Presence

"Dear Lord, bring me into the context of Your world."

1. *Read it*—Remember: We read now only what is there, to hear once again, only what was spoken then. Read John 3:30-32 at least twice, out loud.

2. *Think it*—select a portion, a phrase within the reading, and mull it over in your mind, thinking about the context and setting, reimagining the event, putting yourself into the situation. As you meditate, use all five senses to re-create the context and the setting by building the images that are supplied within the passages.

3. *Pray it*—ask God to give you understanding into how the truths He has spoken in these Scriptures apply to you now. Ask, "What is it about me that I need to deal with? What is it about me that must change?"

   Respond to God by accepting and admitting whatever responsibility is implied by what He has shown. Write what it is that God has shown you, and what you must admit responsibility for having done (or not done).

4. *Live it*—ask God to reveal to you what He wants you to do about what you have admitted.

State what God has revealed that you must admit responsibility for doing.

State what particular action(s) you will take today to accomplish what God has revealed for you to do.

Doing the Discipline: Silence and Solitude

Practicing the Discipline of Silence

Today:

1. Make your conversation full of meaning but not full of words.
   a. Allow others to speak twice as much as you, by listening to them twice as much as you speak.
   b. Do not interrupt others when they are speaking.
   c. Do not think about the next thing you want to say when someone is speaking to you.
   d. Pause for two seconds to think about what you are going to say before you make any reply.
2. Take a fifteen- to thirty-minute silent prayer walk.
   a. Walk alone.
   b. Select a place where you are not likely to be disturbed, somewhere safe, quiet, and as pleasant as possible.
   c. As you walk, ask the Lord, "When have I spoken today when You would have preferred for me to be silent? Why then?"

Journal

Record ideas, impressions, feelings, questions, and any insights you may have had during today's time.

Prayer

Pray for each member of your community.

Give Up the Gods

DAY FIVE

Prayer

Dear Lord, help me to see where I live, work, play, and worship the way You see them, as regions of Your kingdom. Train me to conduct myself according to the rules of Your kingdom rather than of this world's. Teach me to live in them according to Your way. And use me to lead the people of this world to become loyal subjects in Christ's kingdom. Amen.

Core Thought

> To lead as Jesus led we must give up the world's gods, reject its myths and ways, embrace God's kingdom and His truth, and take up Jesus' way.

It is a good starting point to give up the gods of attendance, the need for progress, and the myth of competence. Then we can move on to a new way of being, thinking, and doing. The Jesus way.

Giving up these gods is accomplished by adopting a new way of thinking. Henri Nouwen again helps us:

The way of Christian leadership is not the way of upward mobility in which our world has invested so much, but the way of downward mobility ending on the cross. Here we touch the most important quality of Christian leadership in the future. It is not a leadership of power and control; but a leadership of powerlessness and humility in which the suffering servant of God, Jesus Christ, is made manifest.[6]

As John the Baptist immediately sensed when he saw Jesus, "He must increase, but I must decrease" (John 3:30, NASB). Isn't this freedom when we can lay aside the goals of increased salary, title, prestige, power, and influence? The hardest place to decrease is the influence and power we hold over people around us. Any leadership based on increasing the leader is wrong. But God does give increase and fruit, so by ripping the competitive spirit from our souls, we can see great increase in influence, prestige, and the like, but it is Christ's influence, not ours. Isn't that great? Think of it—whenever people want you to do ministry it is because Christ has increased in you and not because of you.

Leading with our weakness, with our wounds, is a powerful way to touch those around us. We don't lead as a wounded victim but as one who has found an answer in Christ who heals us and enables us to live with and through our needs. It is in this humility that our lives find their real power because God's power becomes mature or perfect in a person's weakness. It is the Jesus way.

Today's Exercises
Core Scripture: 2 Timothy 3:1-17
Read aloud 2 Timothy 3:1-17.
Recite this week's memory verses aloud five times.

> But as for you, continue in what you have learned and have become convinced of, because you know those from whom you learned it, and how from infancy you have known the holy Scriptures, which are able to make you wise for salvation through faith in Christ Jesus. (2 Timothy 3:14-15)

Meditate on today's passage.

---

6. Henri Nouwen, *In the Name of Jesus: Reflection on Christian Leadership* (New York: Crossroad, 1989), 62–63.

Request to Be in His Presence

"Dear Lord, bring me into the context of Your world."

1. *Read it*—Remember: We read now only what is there, to hear once again, only what was spoken then. Read John 3:33-34 at least twice, out loud.

2. *Think it*—select a portion, a phrase within the reading, and mull it over in your mind, thinking about the context and setting, reimagining the event, putting yourself into the situation. As you meditate, use all five senses to re-create the context and the setting by building the images that are supplied within the passages.

3. *Pray it*—ask God to give you understanding into how the truths He has spoken in these Scriptures apply to you now. Ask, "What is it about me that I need to deal with? What is it about me that must change?"

   Respond to God by accepting and admitting whatever responsibility is implied by what He has shown. Write what it is that God has shown you, and what you must admit responsibility for having done (or not done).

4. *Live it*—ask God to reveal to you what He wants you to do about what you have admitted.

State what God has revealed that you must admit responsibility for doing.

State what particular action(s) you will take today to accomplish what God has revealed for you to do.

Doing the Discipline: Silence and Solitude

Practicing the Discipline of Silence

Today:

1. Make your conversation full of meaning but not full of words.
   a. Allow others to speak twice as much as you, by listening to them twice as much as you speak.
   b. Do not interrupt others when they are speaking.
   c. Do not think about the next thing you want to say when someone is speaking to you.
   d. Pause for two seconds to think about what you are going to say before you make any reply.
2. Take a fifteen- to thirty-minute silent prayer walk.
   a. Walk alone.
   b. Select a place where you are not likely to be disturbed, somewhere safe, quiet, and as pleasant as possible.
   c. As you walk, ask the Lord, "When have I spoken today when You would have preferred for me to be silent? Why then?"
3. What was the Lord's answers to the question you asked each day during your silent prayer walk? Write the answers below.

Day One:

Day Two:

Day Three:

Day Four:

Day Five:

Journal

Record ideas, impressions, feelings, questions, and any insights
you may have had during today's time.

Prayer

Pray for each member of your community.

Give Up the Gods

DAY SIX

Community Meeting

In preparation for this week's meeting, you will have read and reflected upon each of the week's five Core Thoughts, recorded your thoughts and observations, and are ready to recite this week's memory verses to the group.

WEEK FOUR

Dedicate Yourself to the Inner Life

DAY ONE

Prayer

Dear Lord, help me to distinguish between my own thoughts and desires and their voices speaking in my head from Yours. I want to know Your will for me each day. But on some days I can't be sure which voice is Yours. Teach me to recognize Your voice speaking within me. I am sorry, Lord. I would have thought by now that I would be able to do such a fundamental thing as knowing Your voice. Amen.

Core Thought

We develop our inner life not by doing things that are about God but by doing the things prompted in us by God, which result from spending extensive time meeting with Him.

Henri Nouwen said, "The central question at the heart of Christian leadership is, are the leaders of the future truly men and women of God, people with an ardent desire to dwell in God's presence, to listen to God's voice, to look at God's beauty, to touch God's incarnate Word, and to taste fully God's infinite goodness?"[1] Notice the range of desires that Nouwen mentions: to dwell, to listen, to focus, and to taste.

These describe a level of experience with God that may be unknown

---

1. Henri Nouwen, *In the Name of Jesus: Reflection on Christian Leadership* (New York: Crossroad, 1989), 29–30.

to many of us, yet is available to anyone who will reserve space in their daily schedule to spend personal time with God. I am not talking now about the typical quiet time, because to be honest, mine were too often just me doing religious stuff with very little experience. I find when I am rushed I fall back into the same superficiality of doing things about God rather than meeting with God.

Being a self-disciplined, well-educated leader with an acceptable quiet time wasn't sufficient to develop the qualities extolled by Henri Nouwen. I had spent thirty years developing my skills and producing many good things, which God had blessed. But I had to submit myself in humility to train to be godly. I needed to be trained in developing my inner life. I made a decision to follow Jesus instead of leading Him. Now my quiet time with God became the training center where I relearned what it meant to follow Jesus.

Today's Exercises
Core Scripture: John 15:1-17
Read aloud John 15:1-17.
Recite this week's memory verse aloud five times.

> I am the good shepherd; I know my sheep and my sheep know me. (John 10:14)

Meditate on today's passage.

Request to Be in His Presence
"Dear Lord, bring me into the context of Your world."

1. **Read it**—Remember: We read now only what is there, to hear once again, only what was spoken then. Read Mark 1:35 at least twice, out loud.
2. **Think it**—select a portion, a phrase within the reading, and mull it over in your mind, thinking about the context and setting, reimagining the event, putting yourself into the situation. As you

meditate, use all five senses to re-create the context and the setting by building the images that are supplied within the passages.

3. *Pray it*—ask God to give you understanding into how the truths He has spoken in these Scriptures apply to you now. Ask, "What is it about me that I need to deal with? What is it about me that must change?"

   Respond to God by accepting and admitting whatever responsibility is implied by what He has shown. Write what it is that God has shown you, and what you must admit responsibility for having done (or not done).

4. *Live it*—ask God to reveal to you what He wants you to do about what you have admitted.

State what God has revealed that you must admit responsibility for doing.

State what particular action(s) you will take today to accomplish what God has revealed for you to do.

Discovering the Discipline: Silence and Solitude

There is something deeply embedded in us that makes silence and solitude, the lying beside still waters motif, seem like loafing. Or at most we consider it a necessary prelude to the real stuff, like an invocation before the championship game. It needs to be done, otherwise the game may not go well for my team. The struggle then is for my core belief to develop parallel to my core behavior. So my core belief must see a connection between what happens when I am with God alone and what happens when I am working for God.

There are two ways to think about this connection. The first would be the pattern of thinking that the longer we pray the more fruit in the ministry. If we fast and pray one day a week, then our churches will grow 20 percent next year instead of 10 percent. We then assume that a successful person must have a devoted prayer life. We make the connection that amounts of prayer make more stuff happen. While this is an attractive idea, this makes spending time with God another church growth technique.

Now I must admit that there is so much mystery in and around prayer that categorical statements about this dimension can't be made. Sometimes there may very well be a correlation between amount of prayer and results. E. M. Bounds said something to the effect that it is not how much we pray but how much of us is in the prayer. It may be that believing, heartfelt prayer is a key. Others might advocate *lectio divina*—a reading of Scripture with the heart so God can speak to you.

Sometimes the real reason we practice spiritual disciplines is less about developing Christ's character in us than it is about accomplishing our ministry and personal goals.

Doing the Discipline: Silence and Solitude

Practicing the Discipline of Silence

Today:

1. Take a fifteen- to thirty-minute silent prayer walk.
   a. Walk alone.
   b. Select a place where you are not likely to be disturbed, somewhere safe, quiet, and as pleasant as possible.
2. As you walk, ask the Lord, "When have I taken the quiet times You wanted to spend with me speaking to me about what matters most to You or simply enjoying each other's presence and used them instead to advance myself and my ministry?"

Journal

Record ideas, impressions, feelings, questions, and any insights you may have had during today's time.

Prayer

Pray for each member of your community.

Dedicate Yourself to the Inner Life

DAY TWO

Prayer

Dear Lord, train Your character into me. Change me into who You want me to be by leading me to do what You want me to do. Today, bring me into opportunities where I can speak words of encouragement and do acts of kindness. Lord, make me holy by training me in doing good. Amen.

Core Thought

> While it is true that who and what we are greatly impacts what we will do, it is also true that what we do greatly impacts who and what we are becoming.

A common construct used to explain the difference between the inner life and the outer life is being and doing. Now it may be true that our doing comes from our being, but we cannot separate the two. In fact, our doing impacts our being because if we pray for God to bless someone we detest, it will change our attitude about the person. In that case doing something transformed our being. But deeds are not paramount to transformation; it is the inner play between the two that makes life work. I like the words of Abraham Joshua Heschel on this subject:

The world needs more than the secret holiness of individual inwardness. It needs more than sacred sentiments and good intentions. God asks for the heart because he needs the lives. It is by lives that the world will be redeemed, by lives that beat in concordance with God, by deeds that outbeat the finite charity of the human heart. *Man's power of action is less vague than his power of intention.* And an action has intrinsic meaning; its value to the world is independent of what it means to the person performing it. The giving of food to a helpless child is meaningful regardless of whether or not the moral intention is present. God asks for the heart, and we must spell our answer in terms of deeds.[2]

It would be safe to say that the claim that purity of heart is the exclusive test of piety is a destructive heresy. It would be just as damaging to believe that actions that are derived from simple human goodness are sufficient to transform the world. It will take a heart response to God to sustain lives of sacrifice. The practical solution for the journey ahead, then, is to *do* something that transforms our being.

Today's Exercises
Core Scripture: John 15:1-17
Read aloud John 15:1-17.
Recite this week's memory verse aloud five times.

> I am the good shepherd; I know my sheep and my sheep know me. (John 10:14)

Meditate on today's passage.

Request to Be in His Presence
"Dear Lord, bring me into the context of Your world."

1. *Read it*—Remember: We read now only what is there, to hear once again, only what was spoken then. Read Matthew 7:21 and

2. Abraham Heschel, "God in Search of Man," in *A Guide to Prayer for Ministers and Other Servants*, comp. Rueben P. Job and Norman Shawchuck (Nashville: Upper Room, 1983), 133.

John 5:14 at least twice, out loud.

2. *Think it*—select a portion, a phrase within the reading, and mull it over in your mind, thinking about the context and setting, reimagining the event, putting yourself into the situation. As you meditate, use all five senses to re-create the context and the setting by building the images that are supplied within the passages.

3. *Pray it*—ask God to give you understanding into how the truths He has spoken in these Scriptures apply to you now. Ask, "What is it about me that I need to deal with? What is it about me that must change?"

    Respond to God by accepting and admitting whatever responsibility is implied by what He has shown. Write what it is that God has shown you, and what you must admit responsibility for having done (or not done).

4. *Live it*—ask God to reveal to you what He wants you to do about what you have admitted.

State what God has revealed that you must admit responsibility for doing.

State what particular action(s) you will take today to accomplish what God has revealed for you to do.

Doing the Discipline: Silence and Solitude

Practicing the Discipline of Silence and Solitude

Today:

1. Take a fifteen- to thirty-minute silent prayer walk.
   a. Walk alone.
   b. Select a place where you are not likely to be disturbed, somewhere safe, quiet, and as pleasant as possible.
2. As you walk, ask the Lord, "When have I taken the quiet times You wanted to spend with me speaking to me about what matters most to You or enjoying each other's presence and used them instead to advance myself and my ministry?"

Journal

Record ideas, impressions, feelings, questions, and any insights you may have had during today's time.

Prayer

Pray for each member of your community.

Dedicate Yourself to the Inner Life

DAY THREE

Prayer

Dear Lord, help me to focus on being obedient to Your calling in my life. Teach me to be completely satisfied by being in Your presence, by having You command me, by doing Your will, and by enjoying being Your child. Amen.

Core Thought

> The primary focus of a spiritual leader is to follow Jesus' way of being and doing.

When the Lord is my Shepherd, my Leader, I will be content. This does not mean passiveness; it means God is in control of the results. I give the effort; He uses it as He pleases. In fact, my personal joy is not based on outcomes; it is based on His love and goodness. I abdicate the responsibility to make things happen. My focus is not primarily to figure out what is happening in my culture or to strategize; it is to follow my Leader's ways of being and doing. My Shepherd is Jesus; He knows my voice, and I know His (John 10:14). The first and most important thing I can do is commit myself to learn how to hear His voice, to enjoy His presence, to experience an intimacy with Him that itself is transformational. This is the part most of us have skipped. We went directly to giving our all for the cause. Amazingly, God loves us and has rewarded us and blessed us in spite of the fact that we have often ignored Him.

So who am I as a leader? I am at the core a follower and one who starts with God. I start with a commitment to dwell, listen, focus, and taste, to dwell in His presence, to listen to His voice, to focus on His beauty, and to taste His goodness. Then there is nothing left to want. All my wanting becomes the flesh rearing its very attractive head. It will on a regular basis. The last thing most of us need to worry about is being impractically passive by spending too much time contemplating God. That impulse, that push to do, is there all the time and it works better when we do from a place of being filled and contented. Then it is sustained and under the Shepherd's control. This then becomes my new engine; it is what is under the hood.

Today's Exercises
Core Scripture: John 15:1-17
Read aloud John 15:1-17.
Recite this week's memory verse aloud five times.

> I am the good shepherd; I know my sheep and my sheep know me. (John 10:14)

Meditate on today's passage.

Request to Be in His Presence
"Dear Lord, bring me into the context of Your world."

1. **Read it**—Remember: We read now only what is there, to hear once again, only what was spoken then. Read John 10:14 at least twice, out loud.
2. **Think it**—select a portion, a phrase within the reading, and mull it over in your mind, thinking about the context and setting, reimagining the event, putting yourself into the situation. As you meditate, use all five senses to re-create the context and the setting by building the images that are supplied within the passages.
3. **Pray it**—ask God to give you understanding into how the truths He has spoken in these Scriptures apply to you now. Ask, "What

is it about me that I need to deal with? What is it about me that must change?"

Respond to God by accepting and admitting whatever responsibility is implied by what He has shown. Write what it is that God has shown you, and what you must admit responsibility for having done (or not done).

4. *Live it*—ask God to reveal to you what He wants you to do about what you have admitted.

State what God has revealed that you must admit responsibility for doing.

State what particular action(s) you will take today to accomplish what God has revealed for you to do.

Doing the Discipline: Silence and Solitude

Practicing the Discipline of Silence and Solitude

Today:

1. Take a fifteen- to thirty-minute silent prayer walk.
   a. Walk alone.
   b. Select a place where you are not likely to be disturbed, somewhere safe, quiet, and as pleasant as possible.
2. As you walk, ask the Lord, "When have I taken the quiet times You wanted to spend with me speaking to me about what matters

most to You or enjoying each other's presence and used them
instead to advance myself and my ministry?"

Journal

Record ideas, impressions, feelings, questions, and any insights
you may have had during today's time.

Prayer

Pray for each member of your community.

Dedicate Yourself to the Inner Life

DAY FOUR

Prayer

Dear Holy Spirit, make Christ so present in me that when those whom I have led stand before Christ, it will not be an altogether new experience. They will have experienced His presence before from having been with me. Amen.

Core Thought

> The primary strength of a spiritual leader is a satisfied soul with which one can lead a powerful life.

The primary strength of a spiritual leader is a satisfied soul with which one can lead a powerful life. On the other hand, to live out of unmet need usually results in dissatisfaction on the part of the leader and the ones he leads.

Pastoral or organizational leaders are trained to make an impact. I (Bill) have spent so much of my life wanting to do better, to accomplish more. My earliest days out of college I was trained to think that God's will is always doing what will reach the most people. Therefore, my decisions were driven by numbers—going to the place where the most people would be touched by my ministry. After years of having quantity as the guiding force of my life when the mission was shrinking rather than growing, where could I go to get my needs met? Good performance gives good rewards, but when the rewards stop, you start running on empty or on fading memories of results in a previous work. So my personal experience was one of dissatisfaction. Either I was seeing results but was driven to see more, or it wasn't going well, and I was in crisis. There was little rest in my soul.

What I have described is very common for leaders. We want, we desire, we claw, and we climb. We have never come to terms with the real source of satisfaction. The interesting thing is that people around us honor this drivenness by calling it holy dissatisfaction.

Leaders don't seem to appreciate what we need the most, but God knows. The primary starting point for a leader who wants to be transformed by God and wants to lead others into the same experience begins with silence and solitude. Our core behavior then is to follow our Leader as He guides us to prayer and reflection, to quietness, and to listening skills that will satisfy and restore our souls. God says, "Lie down here where it is quiet, where I can talk to you, where you can hear what I have to say." This is counterintuitive for the high achiever, so I want to affirm to all high achievers the truth that solitude is action! Solitude is the basic spiritual discipline. Without it you will be hindered in everything else you try. Reading Scripture in spiritual depth is not very effective unless done alone. This practice breaks the back of self-sufficiency—the need to be in control and in the fray. If we give Jesus His way and follow His example, He will say, "Stop here first. Sit a while and let's get on the same page."

Silence and solitude is the best environment for contemplative and deep prayer. There our intimacy with God is deepened, we hear His voice, we learn to enjoy His presence, we taste His goodness and mercy, and He changes our character. As this happens, we understand more about His ways and His means of touching others. Our transformed character begins to touch others in a new way that is attractive. Then more and more people are attracted to how Christ is working in us. So silence and solitude along with other disciplines are the means God uses to transform us. It is by the transformed Christlike character that He has grown within us that His transforming power radiates out from us to those in our sphere of influence. Because it is the character of Christ in us its influence will be stronger and will produce better results than can be produced by our own drivenness and any holy dissatisfaction we may possess.

Today's Exercises

Core Scripture: John 15:1-17

Read aloud John 15:1-17.

Recite this week's memory verse aloud five times.

> I am the good shepherd; I know my sheep and my sheep know me. (John 10:14)

Meditate on today's passage.

Request to Be in His Presence

"Dear Lord, bring me into the context of Your world."

1. **Read it**—Remember: We read now only what is there, to hear once again, only what was spoken then. Read Psalm 23:1 at least twice, out loud.

2. **Think it**—select a portion, a phrase within the reading, and mull it over in your mind, thinking about the context and setting, reimagining the event, putting yourself into the situation. As you meditate, use all five senses to re-create the context and the setting by building the images that are supplied within the passages.

3. **Pray it**—ask God to give you understanding into how the truths He has spoken in these Scriptures apply to you now. Ask, "What is it about me that I need to deal with? What is it about me that must change?"

   Respond to God by accepting and admitting whatever responsibility is implied by what He has shown. Write what it is that God has shown you, and what you must admit responsibility for having done (or not done).

4. **Live it**—ask God to reveal to you what He wants you to do about what you have admitted.

State what God has revealed that you must admit responsibility for doing.

State what particular action(s) you will take today to accomplish what God has revealed for you to do.

Doing the Discipline: Silence and Solitude

Practicing the Discipline of Silence and Solitude

Today:

1. Take a fifteen- to thirty-minute silent prayer walk.
   a. Walk alone.
   b. Select a place where you are not likely to be disturbed, somewhere safe, quiet, and as pleasant as possible.
2. As you walk, ask the Lord, "When have I taken the quiet times You wanted to spend with me speaking to me about what matters most to You or enjoying each other's presence and used them instead to advance myself and my ministry?"

Journal

Record ideas, impressions, feelings, questions, and any insights you may have had during today's time.

Prayer

Pray for each member of your community.

Dedicate Yourself to the Inner Life

DAY FIVE

Prayer

Dear Lord, awaken and refresh me by the vitality of Your presence. Prepare me to lead others by restoring the power of Your everlasting life to my soul. Amen.

Core Thought

> To lead as Jesus led, I must live in obedience to God's commands and direction and submit to His restorative healing of my inner life.

The primary work of a pastor or spiritual leader is to live a life of the restored soul, which comes from time in the green pastures and still waters of His presence. A restored soul is a satisfied soul, and people around us will know it. They will desire the same freedom from spiritual fast food, from slavery to self, from the need to perform in order to fill the emptiness inside. This is the lodestar for the passionate spirituality desperately needed by all of us. It can't be proved with hard data or numerical analysis, but when you experience it, you are transformed.

My Leader or Shepherd, Jesus, has satisfied me. I am not in want of any of the rewards that He finds not worthy to be grasped. My brokenness—which is a state of being, a daily process—provides for me a restored soul. This is why Jesus said we must take up our cross daily and follow Him (Luke 9:23). It is out of this relationship then that I follow His leadership.

These familiar words reach deep within me when I read them: "He makes me to lie down in green pastures; He leads me beside the still waters. He restores my soul" (Psalm 23:2-3, NKJV).

I don't have any personal experience in herding sheep. I only know what I have read, but it makes perfect sense that sheep thrive on certain things. They love pastures of tender green grass and the quiet waters of a small stream. Sheep are easily frightened, and it is in that environment that restoration takes place from the traumas of life. The shepherd knows they need times of rest and nourishment to counterbalance the attacks from other animals and periods of deprivation from food and drink.

God does the same for us. He knows that we need places of nourishment and rest. The pastures God provides never run out of grass, and the streams never run dry.

Other pastures and streams are not satisfying. The other options provide thrills for the soul, but they do not give spiritual nourishment. They are filled with empty promises that damage and disappoint our souls. They numb our souls and lead them away from humility and submission and encourage pride and a take-control attitude. Again Henri Nouwen speaks eloquently to this: "The long painful history of the Church is people ever and again tempted to choose power over love, control over the cross, being a leader over being led."[3] This is what happens when we forget God's character and His ways. The remedy is always to obediently submit to the Gentle Shepherd's leading. He always leads us to rest, healing, fullness, and joy incomparable.

Today's Exercises

Core Scripture: John 15:1-17

Read aloud John 15:1-17.

Recite this week's memory verse aloud five times.

> I am the good shepherd; I know my sheep and my sheep know me. (John 10:14)

---

3. Nouwen, *In the Name of Jesus*, 60.

Meditate on today's passage.

Request to Be in His Presence

"Dear Lord, bring me into the context of Your world."

1. ***Read it***—Remember: We read now only what is there, to hear once again, only what was spoken then. Read Psalm 23:2-3 at least twice, out loud.
2. ***Think it***—select a portion, a phrase within the reading, and mull it over in your mind, thinking about the context and setting, reimagining the event, putting yourself into the situation. As you meditate, use all five senses to re-create the context and the setting by building the images that are supplied within the passages.
3. ***Pray it***—ask God to give you understanding into how the truths He has spoken in these Scriptures apply to you now. Ask, "What is it about me that I need to deal with? What is it about me that must change?"

    Respond to God by accepting and admitting whatever responsibility is implied by what He has shown. Write what it is that God has shown you, and what you must admit responsibility for having done (or not done).
4. ***Live it***—ask God to reveal to you what He wants you to do about what you have admitted.

State what God has revealed that you must admit responsibility for doing.

State what particular action(s) you will take today to accomplish what God has revealed for you to do.

Doing the Discipline: Silence and Solitude
Practicing the Discipline of Silence
Today:

1. Take a fifteen- to thirty-minute silent prayer walk.
   a. Walk alone.
   b. Select a place where you are not likely to be disturbed, somewhere safe, quiet, and as pleasant as possible.
   c. As you walk, ask the Lord, "When have I taken the quiet times You wanted to spend with me speaking to me about what matters most to You or enjoying each other's presence and used them instead to advance myself and my ministry?"
2. What was the Lord's answers to the question you asked each day during your silent prayer walk?
   Write the answers below.

Day One:

Day Two:

Day Three:

Day Four:

Day Five:

Journal

Record ideas, impressions, feelings, questions, and any insights you may have had during today's time.

Prayer

Pray for each member of your community.

Dedicate Yourself to the Inner Life

DAY SIX

Community Meeting

In preparation for this week's meeting, you will have read and reflected upon each of the week's five Core Thoughts, recorded your thoughts and observations, and are ready to recite this week's memory verse to the group.

WEEK FIVE

The Best Leaders Are the Best Followers

DAY ONE

Prayer

Dear Lord, teach me not to think about whether I am up to the task of leading others in Your way. Instead, train me to skip that part and concentrate on doing as Jesus did so that I will become a leader to others in His way, fit to be followed. Amen.

Core Thought

The best leaders are always the best imitators.

Too many people who are leaders in church ministries feel inadequate for the task. I would like to say at the onset that neither adequacy nor inadequacy qualifies or disqualifies someone from doing their part in leading others. Sure, there are skills that make the accomplishment of some tasks more efficient and expertise that allows a job to be done with greater precision, but having a certain skill set or aptitude is not what makes someone an able leader. And lacking these will not keep someone from being an able leader. However, there is one practice to which a believer must be committed to fulfill their duty to lead as Jesus led. They must become excellent in the practice of imitating Christ.

Except for Jesus, the apostle Paul is arguably the best leader the church has ever known. In his letter to the believers of the church in Ephesus, he commands them to "be imitators of God" and to "live a life of love . . . just as Christ" (Ephesians 5:1-2). To the Corinthian believers he urges, "Be imitators of me, just as I also am of Christ" (1 Corinthians 11:1, NASB). He then sends them the young leader "Timothy . . . who is faithful in the Lord" for the specific purpose of reminding them of "my way of life in Christ Jesus, which agrees with what I teach" (1 Corinthians 4:16-17). We see from these passages that:

- All believers are commanded to imitate Christ's life (Ephesians 5:1-2).
- All believers are to lead others to imitate Christ's life (1 Corinthians 11:1).
- Leaders show their faithfulness to Christ by teaching others to imitate His way of life (1 Corinthians 4:16-17).

But what does it mean to imitate Christ?

The apostle Paul chose the Greek word "μιμητής" (*mimētēs* / mim·ay·tace) when he commanded believers to be imitators. Μιμητης (*mimētēs*) is an old word from μιμεομαι (*mimeomai*), meaning to copy, to mimic.[1] From this, we get our English words mimic, mimeograph, and mime. There are two important things to remember about Paul's commandment to "be imitators." First, he is insisting that we constantly reproduce Christ's way of life. Second, Paul is commanding us to exclusively represent Christ's way of life.

That we must constantly reproduce Christ's way of life is indicated by the way Paul said "Be imitators." The grammar he used indicates that he meant "*Keep on* being imitators."[2] Here Paul is saying not only that we must do something, imitate Christ's way of life, he is emphasizing that we must be something, constant reproductions, imitations of Christ. In fact, this was the idea behind the name given to the first believers, "Christian." It meant one who is "a little Christ."

---

1. A. Robertson, "Word Pictures in the New Testament," (1 Corinthians 4:16) *Sunday School Board of the Southern Baptist Convention*, vol. v, 1932 and vol. vi, 1933 (Oak Harbor, WA: Logos Research Systems).

2. For those who are interested in such things: "Keep on becoming (present middle imperative) imitators of me (objective genitive)."

Tomorrow, we will discuss the second thing to remember about Paul's commandment, that we exclusively represent Christ's way of life. For now, we will sum up by recalling that for us to be the best leader to Christ for others, we must, like the apostle Paul and the young leader Timothy, always be the best imitation of Christ before others.

Today's Exercises

Core Scripture: Mark 1:9-21

Read aloud Mark 1:9-21.

Recite this week's memory verse aloud five times.

> Whoever has my commands and obeys them, he is the one who loves me. He who loves me will be loved by my Father, and I too will love him and show myself to him. (John 14:21)

Meditate on today's passage.

Request to Be in His Presence

"Dear Lord, bring me into the context of Your world."

1. **Read it**—Remember: We read now only what is there, to hear once again, only what was spoken then. Read Ephesians 5:1-2 at least twice, out loud.
2. **Think it**—select a portion, a phrase within the reading, and mull it over in your mind, thinking about the context and setting, reimagining the event, putting yourself into the situation. As you meditate, use all five senses to re-create the context and the setting by building the images that are supplied within the passages.
3. **Pray it**—ask God to give you understanding into how the truths He has spoken in these Scriptures apply to you now. Ask, "What is it about me that I need to deal with? What is it about me that must change?"

   Respond to God by accepting and admitting whatever responsibility is implied by what He has shown. Write what it is that God has shown you, and what you must admit responsibility for having done (or not done).

4. *Live it*—ask God to reveal to you what He wants you to do about what you have admitted.

State what God has revealed that you must admit responsibility for doing.

State what particular action(s) you will take today to accomplish what God has revealed for you to do.

Discovering the Discipline: Silence and Solitude

Last week, we said that there were two ways in which the use of the spiritual disciplines can be understood. The first was to view their practice as a necessary precondition to God is causing us and our ministry to be successful. The idea is that the more a leader practices silence and solitude (and the other disciplines, as well) the more God will grow their ministry, make more stuff happen. This makes practicing the disciplines and spending time with God another church growth technique.

The second way to think about silence and solitude is that it is the best environment for contemplative and deep prayer. The practice of these disciplines is not about the growth of ministry but about the transformation of the minister. When our intimacy with God is deepened, we hear His voice, we learn to enjoy His presence, we taste His goodness and mercy, and He changes our character. Through humility and submission we now allow Him to lead us. We understand more about His ways and His means of touching others. So our transformed character begins to touch others in a new way that is attractive. And then more and more people are attracted to how Christ is working in us. We lead with our own brokenness, and the impact is greater.

Silence and solitude along with other disciplines are the means God uses to transform us. A critical change in ethos for the leader is the changing of connections. Think of it as rewiring our connections. Disconnect the wire between a devotional life and numerical results in finance or followers, and reroute it to connect the devotional life to personal character formed by Christ. Then influence comes from Christlike character and radiates out to those in our sphere of influence. That influence will be stronger, and there will be better results because it is the character of Christ in us.

Doing the Discipline: Silence and Solitude

Practicing the Disciplines of Silence and Solitude

Today:

1. Take a fifteen- to thirty-minute silent prayer walk.
   a. Walk alone.
   b. Select a place where you are not likely to be disturbed, somewhere safe, quiet, and as pleasant as possible.
2. As you walk, ask the Lord, "What is it about my character that troubles You the most? That You would like me to address immediately?"

Journal

Record ideas, impressions, feelings, questions, and any insights you may have had during today's time.

Prayer

Pray for each member of your community.

The Best Leaders Are the Best Followers

DAY TWO

Prayer

Dear Lord, help me not to rely on gimmicks to attract people and get them to follow. Make my success in being a leader be measured by how attracted to Christ people become for having been with me. Amen.

Core Thought

> The best leaders are rarely innovators but are usually the best distillers of truth and instillers of confidence.

Yesterday, we learned that all believers are commanded to imitate Christ's life and lead others to imitate Christ's life. Leaders show their faithfulness to Christ by teaching others to imitate His way of life, and that the best leaders are constant imitations of Christ. Today, we will discuss the second thing to remember about Paul's commandment that we "be imitators"; we are to exclusively represent Christ's way of life.

The best leaders are rarely innovators. It is both true and ironic that the best skilled inventors, and the most driven discoverers, are usually the least successful at attracting the interest of others and motivating them to commit to investing in their development. The best at doing so are leaders who *re*-present the big picture truth about living Christ's way of life in smaller life-sized snapshots. By doing this they make it easier for others to get the picture about how they are to live Christ's way. They will imitate Christ by imitating their leader, who is a reproduction, a life-sized re-presentation of Christ. Here lies the important truth for today: The best leaders are rarely innovators. They are usually the best distillers of truth and instillers of confidence.

Those who lead others in Christ's way are called to do nothing other than imitate Christ and imitate *only* Christ. In fact, embedded deep into the very idea of imitation is the requirement that it will immediately call the original back to our minds. To do this the imitator must always display only the qualities that are present in the original, those qualities that make it known, distinguish it, allow it to be recognized, and keep it from being confused with something else. When a leader's way of life presents anything other than (or in addition to) the qualities of Jesus' character, he is always presenting an unfaithful representation. Imitators who fail to be faithful reproductions of Christ alone will also fail to inspire other's confidence in Christ alone because they do not experience the transforming influence of God working in themselves nor do others witness God's transforming power working through them.

Today's Exercises

Core Scripture: Mark 1:9-21

Read aloud Mark 1:9-21.

Recite this week's memory verse aloud five times.

> Whoever has my commands and obeys them, he is the one who loves me. He who loves me will be loved by my Father, and I too will love him and show myself to him. (John 14:21)

Meditate on today's passage.

Request to Be in His Presence

"Dear Lord, bring me into the context of Your world."

1. *Read it*—Remember: We read now only what is there, to hear once again, only what was spoken then. Read 1 Corinthians 11:1-2 at least twice, out loud.

2. *Think it*—select a portion, a phrase within the reading, and mull it over in your mind, thinking about the context and setting,

reimagining the event, putting yourself into the situation. As you meditate, use all five senses to re-create the context and the setting by building the images that are supplied within the passages.

3. *Pray it*—ask God to give you understanding into how the truths He has spoken in these Scriptures apply to you now. Ask, "What is it about me that I need to deal with? What is it about me that must change?"

Respond to God by accepting and admitting whatever responsibility is implied by what He has shown. Write what it is that God has shown you, and what you must admit responsibility for having done (or not done).

4. *Live it*—ask God to reveal to you what He wants you to do about what you have admitted.

State what God has revealed that you must admit responsibility for doing.

State what particular action(s) you will take today to accomplish what God has revealed for you to do.

Doing the Discipline: Silence and Solitude

Practicing the Disciplines of Silence and Solitude

Today:

1. Take a fifteen- to thirty-minute silent prayer walk.
   a. Walk alone.
   b. Select a place where you are not likely to be disturbed, somewhere safe, quiet, and as pleasant as possible.
2. As you walk, ask the Lord, "What is it about my character that troubles You the most? That You would like me to address immediately?"

Journal

Record ideas, impressions, feelings, questions, and any insights you may have had during today's time.

Prayer

Pray for each member of your community.

The Best Leaders Are the Best Followers

DAY THREE

Prayer

Dear Lord, don't let me get distracted by how I will do all the good that I feel can be done. Let my life be focused on doing the one good will that must be done by me "on earth, as it is in heaven." Amen.

Core Thought

> The best leaders have as their top priority being obedient to whatever the Lord commands them to do, doing His will and following in His way.

We rarely appreciate the force behind some of Jesus' statements because their words have become so familiar to us. What's worse, we have most often become familiar with them in almost the worst possible way, through their being read. Either we have read Jesus' words silently to ourselves or someone has read them (usually poorly so) to us. In both cases, we have received them devoid of all the meaning which Jesus' voice inflections, facial expressions, and body language would have conveyed.

We do not know (because we were not present) exactly the way Jesus said what He did. However, there are some statements that thunder out to us with such force that to imagine them being delivered without it is ridiculous and to conceive of them so would border on the irreverent. For example, it is impossible for me to imagine Jesus commanding Lazarus back from the dead with the same forcefulness in His voice an English gentleman would use to thank his guests for their visit: "I say there, Lazarus, my good man! *Do* come back, won't you?" This next example will bring us to my main point.

It is impossible for those who are attentive to Jesus' words to overstate the force with which He must have declared to His disciples what He was commanding them to do in what we now call the Great Commission. Picture the scene: it is after Jesus' resurrection, after His teaching session with Peter and Cleopas on the Emmaus Road, after His appearing to the disciples and then to Thomas the doubter, and after the disciples dined on the miraculous catch of fish. The disciples obeyed Jesus' command, followed His instructions, and proceeded to a mountain in the vicinity of Bethany in Galilee. There, as promised, Jesus appeared to them. Jesus must have thundered, "ALL AUTHORITY IN HEAVEN . . . AND ON EARTH . . . HAS BEEN GIVEN TO ME! . . . THEREFORE . . . GO! NOW! AND MAKE DISCIPLES! YOU TEACH THEM TO OBEY EVERYTHING I HAVE COMMANDED YOU!" (Matthew 28:18-20). The disciples got the message; they were understanding the big picture; it's ALL about obedience.

In the beginning, the disciples obeyed and began to follow Jesus when He called them to become His disciples (Matthew 4:19-20). They obeyed and committed themselves to following Him though most others left (John 6:66-69), and now they obey His command and continue to follow His directions after He has left them (Acts 1:2).

Loving Jesus is all about obedience, following Christ is all about obedience, and leading others is all about being obedient to Christ.

The disciples got it! They were the first and best of Jesus' leaders, and we must imitate their leadership. Their leadership was shaped by their having spent extensive time with their leader, Jesus. During those formative years, they witnessed Jesus' unwavering dedication, His top priority, obedience to His Father's commands, and experienced firsthand the fruit of His transforming influence. They were transformed by the influence of Jesus' character, and by imitating Him they became the best leaders, leaders who wield the power of God's transforming influence.

To best lead others for Christ, we must imitate the best leaders. The best leaders have as their top priority obedience to whatever the Lord commands them to do, doing His will and following in His way. To lead as Jesus led, obedience to His will and following in His way must become our top priority as well.

Today's Exercises
Core Scripture: Mark 1:9-21
Read aloud Mark 1:9-21.
Recite this week's memory verse aloud five times.

> Whoever has my commands and obeys them, he is the one who loves me. He who loves me will be loved by my Father, and I too will love him and show myself to him. (John 14:21)

Meditate on today's passage.

Request to Be in His Presence
"Dear Lord, bring me into the context of Your world."

1. *Read it*—Remember: We read now only what is there, to hear once again, only what was spoken then. Read Acts 21:8-14 at least twice, out loud.
2. *Think it*—select a portion, a phrase within the reading, and mull it over in your mind, thinking about the context and setting, reimagining the event, putting yourself into the situation. As you meditate, use all five senses to re-create the context and the setting by building the images that are supplied within the passages.
3. *Pray it*—ask God to give you understanding into how the truths He has spoken in these Scriptures apply to you now. Ask, "What is it about me that I need to deal with? What is it about me that must change?"

   Respond to God by accepting and admitting whatever responsibility is implied by what He has shown. Write what it is that God has shown you, and what you must admit responsibility for having done (or not done).

4. *Live it*—ask God to reveal to you what He wants you to do about what you have admitted.

State what God has revealed that you must admit responsibility for doing.

State what particular action(s) you will take today to accomplish what God has revealed for you to do.

Doing the Discipline: Silence and Solitude
Practicing the Discipline of Silence
Today:

1. Take a fifteen- to thirty-minute silent prayer walk.
   a. Walk alone.
   b. Select a place where you are not likely to be disturbed, somewhere safe, quiet, and as pleasant as possible.
   c. As you walk, ask the Lord, "What is it about my character that troubles You the most? That You would like me to address immediately?"
2. What was the Lord's answers to the question you asked each day during your silent prayer walk?
   Write the answers on the next page.

Day One:

Day Two:

Day Three:

Journal

Record ideas, impressions, feelings, questions, and any insights you may have had during today's time.

Prayer

Pray for each member of your community.

The Best Leaders Are the Best Followers

DAY FOUR

Prayer

Dear Lord, train me so that the Christlike character You are growing in me will displace all else and provide me with the power to continue Jesus' ministry. Amen.

Core Thought

> The best leaders instill the essence of their ability to lead into people who will continue the process.

Jesus passed on to His disciples the essence of His ability to lead people. The years He spent in their company were training sessions. These were the times when the influence of Jesus' character penetrated so deeply into the disciples' souls that it caused their innermost thoughts and feelings to be revealed. Jesus' influence caused their true beliefs to be revealed. It also revealed to them the essence of Jesus' ability to lead, His total commitment to nothing other than obeying God's will, as God has commanded. But what did the disciples witness Jesus doing as He fulfilled God's commands?

The greatest portion of Jesus' time was spent training the disciples to be His disciples. They witnessed Jesus' obeying God's command-ment to "make disciples" by "training them to obey everything" God had commanded. Jesus was training the disciples to become disciple-makers by being a disciple-maker.

When Jesus knew that the disciples were fully trained in being and making disciples, He said to them,

You are my friends if you do what I command. I no longer call you servants, because a servant does not know his master's business. Instead, I have called you friends, for everything that I learned from my Father I have made known to you. You did not choose me, but I chose you and appointed you to go and bear fruit — fruit that will last. (John 15:14-16)

What is this "fruit that will last" that they are to "go and bear"? The disciples were chosen and appointed to "Go . . . and make disciples" (the Great Commission). The "fruit that will last" is disciples. But not just *any* kind of disciple. The disciples must make disciples "that will last," disciples who continue to make disciple-making disciples. This is the essence of what an able leader is to do.

The best leaders instill the essence of their ability to lead into people who will continue the process. We see this process continuing between the apostle Paul and his disciple, the young church leader named Timothy. Paul commands that "the things you have heard me say in the presence of many witnesses entrust to reliable men who will also be qualified to teach others" (2 Timothy 2:2). The idea that we are to capture is threefold:

1. That a leader must pass on what he learned from his own leader (when he was being trained/discipled by him).
2. That a leader selects who he will train/disciple.
3. That a leader must train only those disciples who are committed to continuing this process of disciple-making.

The disciple-making process is the means by which the best leaders instill the essence of their ability to lead into people who will continue the process.

Today's Exercises

Core Scripture: Mark 1:9-21

Read aloud Mark 1:9-21.

Recite this week's memory verse aloud five times.

> Whoever has my commands and obeys them, he is the one who loves me. He who loves me will be loved by my Father, and I too will love him and show myself to him. (John 14:21)

Meditate on today's passage.

Request to Be in His Presence

"Dear Lord, bring me into the context of Your world."

1. **Read it**—Remember: We read now only what is there, to hear once again, only what was spoken then. Read 2 Timothy 2:2 at least twice, out loud.

2. **Think it**—select a portion, a phrase within the reading, and mull it over in your mind, thinking about the context and setting, reimagining the event, putting yourself into the situation. As you meditate, use all five senses to re-create the context and the setting by building the images that are supplied within the passages.

3. **Pray it**—ask God to give you understanding into how the truths He has spoken in these Scriptures apply to you now. Ask, "What is it about me that I need to deal with? What is it about me that must change?"

   Respond to God by accepting and admitting whatever responsibility is implied by what He has shown. Write what it is that God has shown you, and what you must admit responsibility for having done (or not done).

4. **Live it**—ask God to reveal to you what He wants you to do about what you have admitted.

State what God has revealed that you must admit responsibility for doing.

State what particular action(s) you will take today to accomplish what God has revealed for you to do.

Doing the Discipline: Preparing for a Three-Day Fast
Determining the Purpose of My Fast

This week we will be preparing for the fast that will bring us to the conclusion of the EXPERIENCE THE LIFE course. It is arranged to coordinate with the one-day personal retreat, which is on Day Five of next week. It is a three-day fast that will begin after breakfast on Day Three of next week and conclude with breakfast on Day Six before the final community meeting.

Today, you will begin your preparation by determining the purpose of your fasting. The general purpose of the fast is to prepare your heart, soul, mind, and body to fully experience the Lord's presence and leading during the one-day personal retreat. You, however, will determine the particular issues that you will bring before the Lord, about which you will seek His guidance. You will use this time of fasting to clarify the issues and conform your thinking about them to agree with Christ's. Once you and the Lord are of the same opinion regarding your issues, you will be ready to seek the Lord's guidance as to how He desires you to address them. At the retreat you will be seeking this guidance.

Today, determine the purpose of your fast.

Doing the Discipline: Silence and Solitude
Practicing the Disciplines of Silence and Solitude
Today:
1. Take a fifteen- to thirty-minute silent prayer walk.
    a. Walk alone.
    b. Select a place where you are not likely to be disturbed, some-where safe, quiet, and as pleasant as possible.
    c. As you walk, ask the Lord to direct you in determining the purpose of your fast, about what issues you will be seeking God's directing. Use the questions and your answers from the Doing the Discipline section (on Day Five of weeks One through Four and Day Three of Week Five) to help you determine the issues and the spiritual area in your life that you will be focusing on during the three-day fast.
2. After your walk, briefly describe the issues you will be addressing in your fast, and the outcome you desire (in the space below).

   The purpose of my fast, the issues and outcome I will be focusing on, and about which I will be seeking God's direction are:

Issue:

Outcome:

Issue:

Outcome:

Issue:

Outcome:

Journal

Record ideas, impressions, feelings, questions, and any insights you may have had during today's time.

Prayer

Pray for each member of your community.

The Best Leaders Are the Best Followers

DAY FIVE

Prayer

Dear Lord, bring me to people in whom I can instill the essence of the character You have grown in me. Thank You for the privilege of learning as Your disciple. Amen.

Core Thought

> To lead as Jesus led, you must instill the essence of the character God has grown in you into those who are following your lead.

The very idea that God has chosen each of us to lead others to become like Christ seems extraordinary. In fact, it seems as if it would be an extraordinarily bad idea. Ordinarily this would be true, but we are not dealing with the ordinary when God is dealing with us. Merely ordinary has never been His way (Isaiah 55:8-9). Rather, God's way is to transform something that is ordinary into something extraordinary by using what is ordinary in an extraordinary way. He does this by being present with whatever He desires to transform. It is how God changes the way things are into the way they should be, and it is how God changes us from what we have become into all that He created us to be (1 Corinthians 1:27-29). It stands to reason then that God would use this same way to spread His transforming influence to all the world. And so He has.

God transforms an ordinary sinful man into an extraordinary disciple-making disciple first, by placing His transforming presence within him, and next, by placing him in the presence of his extraordinary leaders, leaders in whom God has grown Christ's character, leaders who wield the power of God's transforming influence. This is God's way, and for this reason He commands us to "remember your leaders, who spoke the word of God to you. Consider the outcome of their way of life and imitate their faith" (Hebrews 13:7).

Today's Exercises
Core Scripture: Mark 1:9-21
Read aloud Mark 1:9-21.
Recite this week's memory verse aloud five times.

> Whoever has my commands and obeys them, he is the one who loves me. He who loves me will be loved by my Father, and I too will love him and show myself to him. (John 14:21)

Meditate on today's passage.

Request to Be in His Presence
"Dear Lord, bring me into the context of Your world."

1. ***Read it***—Remember: We read now only what is there, to hear once again, only what was spoken then. Read Hebrews 13:7 at least twice, out loud.
2. ***Think it***—select a portion, a phrase within the reading, and mull it over in your mind, thinking about the context and setting, reimagining the event, putting yourself into the situation. As you meditate, use all five senses to re-create the context and the setting by building the images that are supplied within the passages.
3. ***Pray it***—ask God to give you understanding into how the truths He has spoken in these Scriptures apply to you now. Ask, "What is it about me that I need to deal with? What is it about me that must change?"

    Respond to God by accepting and admitting whatever

responsibility is implied by what He has shown. Write what it is that God has shown you, and what you must admit responsibility for having done (or not done).

4. ***Live it***—ask God to reveal to you what He wants you to do about what you have admitted.

State what God has revealed that you must admit responsibility for doing.

State what particular action(s) you will take today to accomplish what God has revealed for you to do.

Doing the Discipline: Preparing for a Three-Day Fast
Determining the Privation of My Fast
The second step in preparing for the three-day fast is to determine the *privation* of your fasting, what you will de-*prive* yourself of during your fast. Previously, when you were learning about fasting, we determined from what you would be abstaining. However, from now forward, you will be determining the privation of your fast. Though something having to do with food is usually the thing from which one abstains during a fast, it need not be. You may choose to abstain from an activity of some kind, for instance watching TV, playing sports, reading the newspaper, listening to the radio, talking on your cell phone, or even speaking entirely. The important thing to consider when you choose

the thing from which you are abstaining, is that it must be something that you would ordinarily be doing were you not fasting. It is usually best if you are having trouble with specific issues to choose to abstain from something or an activity that is related to that issue. For example, if you are having difficulty controlling how much you are eating, then abstaining in some way from food during your fast may be very helpful toward surfacing the underlying issues and resolving them.

We are suggesting that you abstain from eating your midday and evening meals, and any in-between snacks for the duration of the fast. You may eat your normal morning meal, but you are to skip the last two meals of the day. During the entirety of the fast you may drink water at any time. You will also be abstaining from watching TV, listening to radio, and other live or recorded forms of commercial communication and entertainment, and the use of the Internet, cell phones, and other electronic devices.[3] You will break your fast with "break-fast" the morning of Day Six of next week. This is only a suggestion. *You* must determine what best serves to prepare you for next week's one-day personal retreat.

Today, determine the form of privation that you will use during the three-day fast.

☐ I will be using the suggested privation. (Check if yes)

If you have decided to use some other form of privation than the one suggested, please describe it below in the space provided. Explain why you chose it.

---

3. Or from whatever deprivation you have chosen.

Doing the Discipline: Silence and Solitude

Practicing the Disciplines of Silence and Solitude

Today take a fifteen- to thirty-minute silent prayer walk.

a. Walk alone.

b. Select a place where you are not likely to be disturbed, somewhere safe, quiet, and as pleasant as possible.

c. As you walk, look for all that is good, and thank the Lord for each good thing. Enjoy!

Journal

Record ideas, impressions, feelings, questions, and any insights you may have had during today's time.

Prayer

Pray for each member of your community.

The Best Leaders Are the Best Followers

DAY SIX

Community Meeting

In preparation for this week's meeting, you will have read and reflected upon each of the week's five Core Thoughts, recorded your thoughts and observations, and are ready to recite this week's memory verse to the group.

WEEK SIX

Give Yourself to the Principle of Discipleship

DAY ONE

Prayer

Dear Lord, I want my life to count for something, something great. There is none greater than You. Lord, I give You my life today. Use it to love others, bring them joy, and give them hope. Amen.

Core Thought

> The kingdom of God is meant to grow through the principle of discipleship.

Christ existed for others. When we take on His form we begin to see the connection between the inner life and the outer life. It is inescapable. If Jesus exists for others, then His followers exist for others and the church community exists for others. It is in this selfless act that we can meet our own needs. When we have changed our mode of leadership, when we begin to minister out of satisfaction rather than want, the Spirit's impulse is to affect others. In fact, I would think anyone filled with God would burst if they couldn't.

The kingdom of God is meant to grow through the principle of discipleship. The principle is the impact of one life on others—the character, skill, and perspective of one godly person passed on to another willing person.

Today's Exercises

Core Scripture: John 4:1-42

Read aloud John 4:1-42.

Recite this week's memory verses aloud five times.

> Therefore go and make disciples of all nations, baptizing them
> in the name of the Father and of the Son and of the Holy Spirit,
> and teaching them to obey everything I have commanded you.
> And surely I am with you always, to the very end of the age.
> (Matthew 28:19-20)

Meditate on today's passage.

Request to Be in His Presence

"Dear Lord, bring me into the context of Your world."

1. ***Read it***—Remember: We read now only what is there, to hear
   once again, only what was spoken then. Read Acts 2:38-41 at
   least twice, out loud.
2. ***Think it***—select a portion, a phrase within the reading, and mull
   it over in your mind, thinking about the context and setting,
   reimagining the event, putting yourself into the situation. As you
   meditate, use all five senses to re-create the context and the setting
   by building the images that are supplied within the passages.
3. ***Pray it***—ask God to give you understanding into how the truths
   He has spoken in these Scriptures apply to you now. Ask, "What
   is it about me that I need to deal with? What is it about me that
   must change?"
   Respond to God by accepting and admitting whatever
   responsibility is implied by what He has shown. Write what it is
   that God has shown you, and what you must admit responsibility
   for having done (or not done).
4. ***Live it***—ask God to reveal to you what He wants you to do
   about what you have admitted.

State what God has revealed that you must admit responsibility for doing.

State what particular action(s) you will take today to accomplish what God has revealed for you to do.

Discovering the Discipline: Silence and Solitude

The experience of silence and solitude will restore our souls (Psalm 23:3). The Hebrew word for restore means "to bring it back." One must ask where it has been. It has been wandering and found other places for rest and comfort. Isn't this what happens to us when we lose our closeness to God by not spending time with Him? We get away from the green pastures and still waters where the soul's sustenance resides. The other pastures and streams are not satisfying. The other options provide thrills for the soul, but they do not give spiritual nourishment. They are filled with empty promises that damage and disappoint our souls. They numb our souls and lead them away from humility and submission and encourage pride and a take-control attitude. Again Henri Nouwen speaks eloquently to this: "The long painful history of the Church is people ever and again tempted to choose power over love, control over the cross, being a leader over being led."[1] This is what happens when we

---

1. Henri Nouwen, *In the Name of Jesus: Reflection on Christian Leadership* (New York: Crossroad, 1989), 60.

forget God's character and His ways. If we are praised for our achievements in ministry, we can be in danger of our souls feeding in the pasture of adulation and ego gratification. We drink the waters of self-importance and start grasping for that which Christ did not grasp.

If we become accustomed to adulation, then not to be mentioned or acknowledged causes a wound and can lead to anger and a sarcastic spirit toward the evangelical fame machine. Affirmation can be a wonderful thing, but if we come to expect praise, it may require a significant time in God's pasture drinking the right water in order to restore the damage done.

Doing the Discipline: Preparing for the Three-Day Fast
Dedicating My Physical Self to God

In this third step of preparing for the fast, you will dedicate your physical self, your body and its feelings and actions as a living sacrifice to God.

Keeping your purpose in mind, write a prayer dedicating your body, its strength, health, and comfort as a sacrifice to God. Acknowledge that He is the one who provides for your body, and state what it is that He provides for it. Tell Him why you are giving Him this time of fasting and that you give it freely, whether your purpose is fulfilled or not. Tell Him that what you desire more than the fulfilling of your purpose is to enjoy this time in His presence.

My Prayer of Dedication to You, Lord:

Doing the Discipline: Silence and Solitude

Practicing the Discipline of Silence and Solitude

Today:

1. Pray your Prayer of Dedication.
2. Take a fifteen- to thirty-minute silent prayer walk.
   a. Walk alone.
   b. Select a place where you are not likely to be disturbed, somewhere safe, quiet, and as pleasant as possible.
   c. As you walk, look for all that is good, and thank the Lord for each good thing. Enjoy!

Journal

Record ideas, impressions, feelings, questions, and any insights you may have had during today's time.

Prayer

Pray for each member of your community.

Give Yourself to the Principle of Discipleship

DAY TWO

Prayer

Dear Lord, help me to remain available for others so that others can experience You through me anytime You desire. Amen.

Core Thought

> The command and the curriculum is "teaching them to obey everything I commanded you."

The command and curriculum is "teaching them to obey everything I commanded you" (Matthew 28:20). Jesus commanded 212 things, which provides us with a very rich curriculum. The aim of the teaching is obedience, which should encourage those of us who believe that faith is action sustained by belief.

But the curriculum is not only everything Jesus commanded but also everything He did and the way He lived. How Jesus lived taught the disciples and teaches us that:

1. A disciple submits to a teacher who teaches him or her how to follow Jesus.
2. A disciple learns Jesus' words.
3. A disciple learns Jesus' way of ministry.
4. A disciple imitates Jesus' life and character.
5. A disciple finds and teaches other disciples.

As leaders we cannot be satisfied with just talking about what Jesus commanded or did or the way in which He did them. We must be committed to living it out in community with others. "For this is the love of God, that we keep his commandments. And his commandments are not burdensome" (1 John 5:3, RSV).

Today's Exercises

Core Scripture: John 4:1-42
Read aloud John 4:1-42.
Recite this week's memory verses aloud five times.

> Therefore go and make disciples of all nations, baptizing them in the name of the Father and of the Son and of the Holy Spirit, and teaching them to obey everything I have commanded you. And surely I am with you always, to the very end of the age. (Matthew 28:19-20)

Meditate on today's passage.

Request to Be in His Presence

"Dear Lord, bring me into the context of Your world."

1. **Read it**—Remember: We read now only what is there, to hear once again, only what was spoken then. Read 1 Peter 1:3 at least twice, out loud.
2. **Think it**—select a portion, a phrase within the reading, and mull it over in your mind, thinking about the context and setting, reimagining the event, putting yourself into the situation. As you meditate, use all five senses to re-create the context and the setting by building the images that are supplied within the passages.
3. **Pray it**—ask God to give you understanding into how the truths He has spoken in these Scriptures apply to you now. Ask, "What is it about me that I need to deal with? What is it about me that must change?"

Respond to God by accepting and admitting whatever responsibility is implied by what He has shown. Write what it is that God has shown you, and what you must admit responsibility for having done (or not done).

4. *Live it*—ask God to reveal to you what He wants you to do about what you have admitted.

State what God has revealed that you must admit responsibility for doing.

State what particular action(s) you will take today to accomplish what God has revealed for you to do.

Doing the Discipline: Preparing for the Three-Day Fast
Directing My Spirit's Passions Toward God
Tomorrow after breakfast you will begin your three-day fast. Today we will take the final step in preparing for it, directing your spirit's passion toward God.

Today:
1. List below the first three personal aspirations and personal goals that come to your mind.

My personal aspirations and goals:

2. Pray, asking God to direct your passions toward Him.
   a. Ask God to help you lay aside whatever agenda you may have for meeting the needs represented on your list.
   b. Ask Him to guide you through the journey of making His will the main passion in your life.
   c. Ask Him to use this time to train you to trust in Him.

Doing the Discipline: Silence and Solitude
Practicing the Discipline of Silence and Solitude Today:

1. Pray your Prayer of Dedication.
2. Take a fifteen- to thirty-minute silent prayer walk.
   a. Walk alone.
   b. Select a place where you are not likely to be disturbed, somewhere safe, quiet, and as pleasant as possible.
   c. As you walk, look for all that is good, and thank the Lord for each good thing. Enjoy!

Journal

Record ideas, impressions, feelings, questions, and any insights you may have had during today's time.

Prayer

Pray for each member of your community.

Give Yourself to the Principle of Discipleship

DAY THREE

Prayer

Dear Lord, help me to keep my priorities in order. I have a tendency to work so hard at doing something well that I will forget the real good that You intended in the first place. I often confuse doing something well with doing something good. Thank You for the people You have placed in my life who keep me accountable to do the good things You have commanded. Amen.

Core Thought

> We are to live out Jesus' commands in a community
> of grace in which there is a common commitment
> to follow Jesus and help others to do the same.

Because character is developed in community, you can't make disciples without accountability. That accountability should be relationships of trust in an environment of grace. Accountability without trusting relationships will feel militaristic and will not last long. Unless there are relationships of trust, our unresolved sin, guilt, and shame will dive deeper into the hidden places of our souls where they will remain unhealed and will resurface later in damaging ways.

Discipleship that is lived out in community provides a balance of time alone with God and time with others. They work together and, in fact, are of equal importance. We are to live out Jesus' commands in a community of grace in which there is a common commitment to follow Jesus and to help others to do the same. Following is a representative list of His commands:

> Love one another as I have loved you (John 13:34-35).
> Bless those who persecute you (Matthew 5:11-12).
> Esteem one another (1 Thessalonians 5:13).
> Comfort one another (1 Thessalonians 5:14).
> Forgive one another (Matthew 6:12,15).
> Confess your sins to one another (James 5:16).
> Agree in prayer with each other (Matthew 18:19-20).
> Love your neighbor (Matthew 22:39).

Finally, we are commanded to "encourage one another daily, as long as it is called Today, so that none of you may be hardened by sin's deceitfulness" (Hebrews 3:13), and to "encourage one another—and all the more" to "spur one another on toward love and good deeds," and to "not give up meeting together" (Hebrews 10:24-25).

It is in this way that we share our common commitment to follow Jesus, and help others to do the same.

Today's Exercises
Core Scripture: John 4:1-42
Read aloud John 4:1-42.
Recite this week's memory verses aloud five times.

> Therefore go and make disciples of all nations, baptizing them
> in the name of the Father and of the Son and of the Holy Spirit,
> and teaching them to obey everything I have commanded you.
> And surely I am with you always, to the very end of the age.
> (Matthew 28:19-20)

Meditate on today's passage.

Request to Be in His Presence
"Dear Lord, bring me into the context of Your world."

1. **Read it**—Remember: We read now only what is there, to hear once again, only what was spoken then. Read 1 Peter 1:3 at least twice, out loud.

2. **Think it**—select a portion, a phrase within the reading, and mull it over in your mind, thinking about the context and setting, reimagining the event, putting yourself into the situation. As you meditate, use all five senses to re-create the context and the setting by building the images that are supplied within the passages.

3. **Pray it**—ask God to give you understanding into how the truths He has spoken in these Scriptures apply to you now. Ask, "What is it about me that I need to deal with? What is it about me that must change?"

   Respond to God by accepting and admitting whatever responsibility is implied by what He has shown. Write what it is that God has shown you, and what you must admit responsibility for having done (or not done).

4. **Live it**—ask God to reveal to you what He wants you to do about what you have admitted.

State what God has revealed that you must admit responsibility for doing.

State what particular action(s) you will take today to accomplish what God has revealed for you to do.

Doing the Discipline: Silence and Solitude

Practicing the Discipline of Silence and Solitude

Today:

1. Pray your Prayer of Dedication.
2. Take a fifteen- to thirty-minute silent prayer walk.
   a. Walk alone
   b. Select a place where you are not likely to be disturbed, somewhere safe, quiet, and as pleasant as possible.
   c. As you walk, look for all that is good, and thank the Lord for each good thing. Enjoy!

Doing the Discipline: Executing the Three-Day Fast

Executing the Three-Day Fast

Beginning after breakfast and continuing until the morning of Day Six, you will abstain from eating your midday and evening meals and any in-between snacks.[2] You may eat your normal morning meal, but you are to skip the last two meals of the day. During the entirety of the fast you may drink water, at any time. You will also be abstaining from watching TV, listening to radio, and other live or recorded forms of commercial communication and entertainment. You will break your fast with "break-fast" the morning of Day Six of this week.

Documenting My Perspective During My Fasting

Use the space below to journal today's experiences as you begin your fast.

Record ideas, impressions, feelings, questions, and any insights you may have had during today's time.

---

2. Or from whatever deprivation you have chosen.

Prayer

Pray for each member of your community.

Give Yourself to the Principle of Discipleship

DAY FOUR

Prayer

Dear Lord, give me the strength of character to keep my commitment to being trained in Your way and to train others in Your way. Amen.

Core Thought

> The command is to be and make disciples, and the method is tried and true: Teach faithful people who in turn will be able to teach others.

The command is to be and make disciples, which means "teaching them to obey everything I commanded you" (Matthew 28:20). The method is tried and true: "Teach faithful people who in turn will be able to teach others" (2 Timothy 2:2). This means that as a leader I will choose to invest my best effort in developing faithful leaders who will be able to reproduce. This also means that a good deal of my time could be spent meeting with a few in order to have a larger impact later.

It has been my belief for many years that it is the neglect of this simple process that is behind our weakness as a church. This neglect has been largely due to pastors and other leaders not having the patience and commitment to the process. It is too tempting to build a large congregation faster through preaching. For those who can draw large crowds, there are very tangible rewards in being known as a great communicator.

Our behavior reveals what we really care about, and sadly, in too many cases that is success in numbers and recognition of our skills.

This must be cast off and abandoned by those leaders who want to follow Jesus. We should keep preaching and strategizing the best we can, but we must put our best effort into the training of faithful leaders. Training seminars and occasional leadership retreats don't cut it. It must be a sustained effort one-on-one or in groups of three or four in order to develop the best results. Listen to Paul's advice to Timothy and to the Philippian believers:

> Now you have observed my teaching, my conduct, my aim in life, my faith, my patience, my love, my steadfastness, my persecutions, my sufferings, what befell me at Antioch, at Iconium, and at Lystra, what persecutions I endured; yet from them all the Lord rescued me . . . But as for you, continue in what you have learned and firmly believed, *knowing from whom you have learned it.* (2 Timothy 3:10,14, RSV, emphasis added)

And Paul also writes, "What you have learned and received and heard and seen in me, do; and the God of peace will be with you" (Philippians 4:9, RSV). These passages scream relationship, doing the work together, spending time together, knowing each other intimately. I often think of the words of Elton Trueblood when it comes to this kind of investment:

> There is no person in history who has impacted all of mankind more than Jesus of Nazareth. Jesus was deeply concerned for the continuation of his redemptive, reconciling work after the close of his earthly existence, and his chosen method was the formation of a small band of committed friends. He did not form an army, establish a headquarters, or even write a book. What he did was to collect a few very common men and women, inspire them with the sense of his spirit and vision, and build their lives into an intensive fellowship of affection, worship and work.
>
> One of the truly shocking passages of the gospel is that

in which Jesus indicates that there is absolutely no substitute for the tiny, loving, caring, reconciling society. If this fails, he suggests, all is failure; there is no other way. He told the little bedraggled fellowship that they were actually the salt of the earth and that if this salt should fail there would be no adequate preservative at all. He was staking all on one throw.

What we need is not intellectual theorizing or even preaching, but a demonstration. One of the most powerful ways of turning people's loyalty to Christ is by loving others with the great love of God. We cannot revive faith by argument, but we might catch the imagination of puzzled men and women by an exhibition of a fellowship so intensely alive that every thoughtful person would be forced to respect it. If there should emerge in our day such a fellowship, wholly without artificiality and free from the dead hand of the past, it would be an exciting event of momentous importance. A society of genuine loving friends, set free from the self-seeking struggle for personal prestige and from all unreality, would be something unutterably priceless and powerful. A wise person would travel any distance to join it.[3]

Today's Exercises

Core Scripture: John 4:1-42

Read aloud John 4:1-42.

Recite this week's memory verses aloud five times.

Therefore go and make disciples of all nations, baptizing them in the name of the Father and of the Son and of the Holy Spirit, and teaching them to obey everything I have commanded you. And surely I am with you always, to the very end of the age. (Matthew 28:19-20)

---

3. Excerpts from James R. Newby, *Best of Elton Trueblood* (Nashville: Impact Books, 1979), throughout.

Meditate on today's passage.

Request to Be in His Presence

"Dear Lord, bring me into the context of Your world."

1. *Read it*—Remember: We read now only what is there, to hear once again, only what was spoken then. Read 1 Peter 1:3 at least twice, out loud.

2. *Think it*—select a portion, a phrase within the reading, and mull it over in your mind, thinking about the context and setting, reimagining the event, putting yourself into the situation. As you meditate, use all five senses to re-create the context and the setting by building the images that are supplied within the passages.

3. *Pray it*—ask God to give you understanding into how the truths He has spoken in these Scriptures apply to you now. Ask, "What is it about me that I need to deal with? What is it about me that must change?"

   Respond to God by accepting and admitting whatever responsibility is implied by what He has shown. Write what it is that God has shown you, and what you must admit responsibility for having done (or not done).

4. *Live it*—ask God to reveal to you what He wants you to do about what you have admitted.

State what God has revealed that you must admit responsibility for doing.

State what particular action(s) you will take today to accomplish what God has revealed for you to do.

Doing the Discipline: Silence and Solitude
Practicing the Discipline of Silence and Solitude
Today:

1. Pray your Prayer of Dedication.
2. Take a fifteen- to thirty-minute silent prayer walk.
   a. Walk alone.
   b. Select a place where you are not likely to be disturbed, somewhere safe, quiet, and as pleasant as possible.
   c. As you walk, look for all that is good, and thank the Lord for each good thing. Enjoy!

Doing the Discipline: Executing the Three-Day Fast
Documenting My Perspective During My Fasting
Use the space below to journal today's experiences as you continue your fast.

Record ideas, impressions, feelings, questions, and any insights you may have had during today's time.

Prayer

Pray for each member of your community.

Give Yourself to the Principle of Discipleship

DAY FIVE

The One-Day Personal Retreat

Start your retreat by:

- Asking the Lord to make you aware of His presence during every minute and activity of your retreat,
- Enjoying your breakfast alone,
- Doing today's Experience the Life readings and exercises.

Prayer

Dear Lord, I want You to continue to make me more like Jesus. I don't want to waste any more of my life daydreaming about being like Jesus. I want the reality of His life living in me daily. Father, I make it my intention to become so like Jesus that were it not for Your limitless knowledge and unsurpassable wisdom, even You would have a hard time telling us apart. I'm in this process for the long haul. Thanks for being here with me. Amen.

Core Thought

> To lead as Jesus led, you must give to others
> Christ who is in you and teach them to follow
> Him as you have learned to follow Him.

What Jesus taught and modeled, which was imitated by Paul with Timothy and others, is the most powerful force for change. It is the influence of one person's character on another. As Henri Nouwen said, "The greatest gift I have to offer is my own joy of living, my own inner peace, my own silence and solitude, my own sense of well-being."[4] As Trueblood put it, "A wise person would travel any distance to join it."[5] Peter did, John did, Matthew did, Timothy did, Titus did, Luke did, and many of you reading this book did. There is nothing like it anywhere—the power of a transformed life.

This is the reason the principle of discipleship is God's way to reach the world. In fact it is the only way to reach the world. God has put each of us into the middle of the harvest field as insiders so our lives can speak to those around us. That is the way the kingdom is to grow, through the natural means of one life on another. This gets at the heart of this book's thesis: A transformed life is needed, a life of depth of true disciples who have chosen to follow the life that Jesus lived. The reason the mission languishes is the acceptance of a non-discipleship Christianity that creates shallow believers with hollow lives who don't affect those around them. This has led to the marginalization of the gospel and has retarded its spread because of its lack of authenticity and power.

Today's Exercises

Core Scripture: John 4:1-42

Read aloud John 4:1-42.

Recite this week's memory verses aloud five times.

> Therefore go and make disciples of all nations, baptizing them
> in the name of the Father and of the Son and of the Holy Spirit,
> and teaching them to obey everything I have commanded you.
> And surely I am with you always, to the very end of the age.
> (Matthew 28:19-20)

Meditate on today's passage.

---

4. Henri Nouwen, *The Life of the Beloved* (New York: Crossroad, 1992), 90.

5. Elton Trueblood, "A Radical Experiment," William Penn Lectures delivered in 1947 at the Arch Street Meeting House, Philadelphia, http://www.quaker.org/pamphlets/wpl1947a.html.

Request to Be in His Presence

"Dear Lord, bring me into the context of Your world."

1. ***Read it***—Remember: We read now only what is there, to hear once again, only what was spoken then. Read 1 Peter 1:3 at least twice, out loud.

2. ***Think it***—select a portion, a phrase within the reading, and mull it over in your mind, thinking about the context and setting, reimagining the event, putting yourself into the situation. As you meditate, use all five senses to re-create the context and the setting by building the images that are supplied within the passages.

3. ***Pray it***—ask God to give you understanding into how the truths He has spoken in these Scriptures apply to you now. Ask, "What is it about me that I need to deal with? What is it about me that must change?"

   Respond to God by accepting and admitting whatever responsibility is implied by what He has shown. Write what it is that God has shown you, and what you must admit responsibility for having done (or not done).

4. ***Live it***—ask God to reveal to you what He wants you to do about what you have admitted.

State what God has revealed that you must admit responsibility for doing.

State what particular action(s) you will take today to accomplish what God has revealed for you to do.

Deriving the Profit from My Fasting

Start by reviewing the journal entries that you made on days Three and Four of this week during your time of fasting:

1. Read each statement and ask yourself, "What did I mean when I wrote this down?"
2. Using the space below, answer the question,

"What did I experience?"

"What do I know now from these experiences?"

3. Ask the Lord the following questions and write whatever comes to your mind as the result.

"Lord, what do you want me to learn from these experiences?"

"Lord, what do you want me to do with what I now know?"

4. Write a short summary of what you have experienced, thus far, preparing and executing your three-day fast.

5. List the issues that the Lord impressed upon you. What is it about your current character that needs to change? What do you need to know from the Lord about making these changes? These will be used in today's retreat.

6. Write a short statement of what you learned and what you believe God is leading you to do thus far, with what you have learned from your fast.

Doing the Discipline: Silence and Solitude
Practicing the Discipline of Silence and Solitude
1. Take a thirty-minute silent prayer walk.
   a. Walk alone.
   b. Select a place where you are not likely to be disturbed, somewhere safe, quiet, and as pleasant as possible.
   c. As you walk, look for all that is good, and thank the Lord for each good thing. Enjoy!
2. When you return from your walk, read *The Depths*, and follow Jeanne Guyon's instructions. Slowly pray and perform the commands that are italicized in silence.

The Depths: a meditation

The first thing you must learn, dear friend, is that "the kingdom of God is within you" (Luke 17:21).

Never look for the kingdom anywhere but there, within. Once you have realized that the kingdom of God is within you and can be found there, just come to the Lord.

As you come, come with a deep sense of love; come to Him very gently; come to Him with a deep sense of worship.

As you come to Him, humbly acknowledge that He is everything. Confess to Him that you are nothing.

Close your eyes to everything around you; begin to open the inward eyes of your soul, turning those eyes to your spirit.

In a word, *give your full attention* to the deep inward parts of your being.

You need only *believe that God dwells in you*. This belief, and this belief alone, will bring you into His holy presence.

Do not allow your mind to wander about but hold it in submission as much as possible.

Once you are in the Lord's presence, *be still and quiet* before Him.

And now, there in His presence, simply begin to *repeat the Lord's Prayer*.

Begin with the word, *"Father."* As you do, let the full meaning of that word deeply touch your heart.

Believe that the God who lives inside you is indeed so willing to be your Father.

Pour out your heart to Him as a little child pours out his heart to his father.

Never doubt your Lord's deep love for you.

Never doubt His desire to hear you.

Call on His name and remain before Him silently for a little while.

Remain there, waiting to have His heart made known to you.

As you come to Him, come as a weak child, one who is all soiled and badly bruised—a child that has been hurt from falling again and again.

Come to the Lord as one who has no strength of his own; come to Him as one who has no power to cleanse himself.

Humbly lay your pitiful condition before your Father's gaze.

While you wait there before Him, occasionally utter a word of love to Him and a word of grief over your sin. Then simply wait for a while.

[After waiting, you will sense when it is time to go on; when that moment comes, simply continue on in the Lord's Prayer.]

As you speak the words, "Thy Kingdom come," call upon your Lord, the King of Glory, to reign in you.

Give yourself up to God. *Give yourself* to God so that He may do in your heart what you have so long been a failure in trying to do.

Acknowledge before Him His right to rule over you.

[At some point in this encounter with your Lord, you will feel deep within your spirit that it is time to simply remain silent before Him. When you have such a sense, do not move on to the next word—not as long as this sense continues with you. You see, it is the Lord Himself who is holding you to silence. When that sense of waiting before Him has passed,]

Go on again to the next words of the Lord's Prayer.

"Your will be done on earth as it is in heaven."

Praying these words, humble yourself before the Lord, earnestly *asking Him* to accomplish His whole will in you and through you.

Surrender your heart into His hands. *Surrender your freedom* into His hands. *Yield to your Lord* His right to do with you as He pleases.

Do you know what God's will is? His will is that His children love Him. Therefore, when you pray, "Lord, Your will be done," you are actually asking the Lord to allow you to love Him.

So begin to love Him! And as you do, beseech Him to give you His love.

[There is no need for using repetition or memorized prayers.

Instead, simply repeat the Lord's Prayer as I have here described. It will produce abundant fruit in your life.]

Dear child of God, all your concepts of what God is like really amount to nothing. Do not try to imagine what God is like. Instead, simply believe in His presence. Never try to imagine what God will do. There is no way God will ever fit into your concepts.

What then shall you do? Seek to behold Jesus Christ by looking to Him in your inmost being, in your spirit.

When the presence of the Lord really becomes your experience, you will actually discover that you have gradually begun to love this silence and peaceful rest which come with His presence. There is a wonderful enjoyment of His presence.[6]

3. After you have finished meditating and reading, take a ten-minute silent stretch-your-legs walk.

   a. Walk alone.

   b. Select a place where you are not likely to be disturbed, somewhere safe, quiet, and as pleasant as possible.

   c. As you walk, breath deeply, and stretch your arms and legs. Remember to drink plenty of water.

4. After your walk, retrieve the list of issues you composed earlier today (from *Deriving the Profit from My Fasting*, question 5).

   a. Take each issue in turn.

   b. Ask the Lord to reveal to you how He would like for you to make the needed changes in your character.

   [DO NOT RUSH. Wait to hear from the Lord. If a long period passes with no apparent answer, then ask the Lord several questions about the issue. Remember, the Lord probably will not answer about how you should make the needed changes to your character until you are in agreement with Him about your need to change. Like-mindedness with the Father must always precede partnership with His Son.]

6. Jeanne Guyon, *Experiencing the Depths of Jesus Christ* (Auburn, ME: Seedsowers, 1975), 15–19.

   c. Write the issue about your character that must change, and the way the Lord would like you to go about changing it.

Character Issues and Changes to Make

5. After you have finished praying and writing, take a twenty-minute silent rest-your-brain walk.
   a. Walk alone.
   b. Select a place where you are not likely to be disturbed, somewhere safe, quiet, and as pleasant as possible.
   c. As you walk, breath deeply, and stretch your arms and legs.
   d. Don't try to think on anything in particular, just relax. Remember to drink plenty of water.
6. After your walk, read the following excerpt from C. S. Lewis's *Screwtape Letters*.[7] It is written by an experienced demon-tempter (named Screwtape) to his nephew (Wormwood), a novice tempter. Screwtape is giving his nephew expert advice on how to cause Christians to cease following Christ ("the Enemy"). Enjoy!

MY DEAR WORMWOOD,

So you "have great hopes that the patient's religious phase is dying away," have you? I always thought the Training College had gone to pieces since they put old Slubgob at the head of it, and now I am sure. Has no one ever told you about the law of Undulation?

Humans are amphibians—half spirit and half animal. (The Enemy's determination to produce such a revolting hybrid was one of the things that determined Our Father to withdraw his support from Him.) As spirits they belong to the eternal world, but as animals they inhabit time. This means that while their spirit can he directed to an eternal object, their bodies, passions, and imaginations are in continual change, for to be in time means to change. Their nearest approach to constancy, therefore, is undulation—the

---

7. C. S. Lewis, *The Screwtape Letters with Screwtape Proposes a Toast* (New York: Macmillan, 1961), 44–47.

repeated return to a level from which they repeatedly fall back, a series of troughs and peaks. If you had watched your patient carefully you would have seen this undulation in every department of his life—his interest in his work, his affection for his friends, his physical appetites, all go up and down. As long as he lives on earth periods of emotional and bodily richness and liveliness will alternate with periods of numbness and poverty. The dryness and dullness through which your patient is now going are not, as you fondly suppose, your workmanship; they are merely a natural phenomenon which will do us no good unless you make a good use of it.

To decide what the best use of it is, you must ask what use the Enemy wants to make of it, and then do the opposite. Now it may surprise you to learn that in His efforts to get permanent possession of a soul, He relies on the troughs even more than on the peaks; some of His special favorites have gone through longer and deeper troughs than anyone else. The reason is this. To us a human is primarily food; our aim is the absorption of its will into ours, the increase of our own area of selfhood at its expense. But the obedience which the Enemy demands of men is quite a different thing. One must face the fact that all the talk about His love for men, and His service being perfect freedom, is not (as one would gladly believe) mere propaganda, but an appalling truth. He really does want to fill the universe with a lot of loathsome little replicas of Himself—creatures whose life, on its miniature scale, will be qualitatively like His own, not because He has absorbed them but because their wills freely conform to His. We want cattle who can finally become food; He wants servants who can finally become sons. We want to suck in, He wants to give out. We are empty and would be filled; He is full and flows over. Our war aim is a world in which Our Father Below has drawn all other beings into himself: the Enemy wants a world full of beings united to Him but still distinct.

And that is where the troughs come in. You must have often wondered why the Enemy does not make more use of His power to be sensibly present to human souls in any degree He chooses and at any moment. But you now see that the Irresistible and the Indisputable are the two weapons which the very nature of His scheme forbids Him to use. Merely to override a human will (as His felt presence in any but the faintest and most mitigated degree would certainly do) would be for Him useless. He cannot ravish. He can only woo. For His ignoble idea is to eat the cake and have it; the creatures are to be one with Him, but yet themselves; merely to cancel them, or assimilate them, will not serve. He is prepared to do a little overriding at the beginning. He will set them off with communications of His presence which, though faint, seem great to them, with emotional sweetness, and easy conquest over temptation. But He never allows this state of affairs to last long. Sooner or later He withdraws, if not in fact, at least from their conscious experience, all those supports and incentives. He leaves the creature to stand up on its own legs—to carry out from the will alone duties which have lost all relish. It is during such trough periods, much more than during the peak periods, that it is growing into the sort of creature He wants it to be. Hence the prayers offered in the state of dryness are those which please Him best. We can drag our patients along by continual tempting, because we design them only for the table, and the more their will is interfered with the better. He cannot "tempt" to virtue as we do to vice. He wants them to learn to walk and must therefore take away His hand; and if only the will to walk is really there He is pleased even with their stumbles. Do not be deceived, Wormwood. Our cause is never more in danger than when a human, no longer desiring, but still intending, to do our Enemy's will, looks round upon a universe from which every trace of Him seems to have vanished, and asks why he has been forsaken, and still obeys.

But of course the troughs afford opportunities to our side also. Next week I will give you some hints on how to exploit them,

Your affectionate uncle
SCREWTAPE

Use the remaining time to journal and pray.

Journal

Record ideas, impressions, feelings, questions, and any insights you may have had during today's time.

Prayer

Spend extended time praying for your family, friends, and for each member of your EXPERIENCE THE LIFE community.

Give Yourself to the Principle of Discipleship

DAY SIX

Doing the Discipline: Breaking Your Fast

Deriving the Profit from My Fasting

Start by reviewing the journal entries that you made yesterday:

1. Read each statement and ask yourself, "What did I mean when I wrote this down?"
2. Using the space below, answer the question

"What did I experience?"

"What do I know now, from these experiences?"

3. Ask the Lord the following questions and write whatever comes to your mind as the result.

"Lord, what do you want me to learn from these experiences?"

"Lord, what do you want me to do with what I now know?"

4. Write a short statement of what you learned and what you believe God is leading you to do with what you have learned from your fast about your current character and what you need to do to further shape it into Christ's.

5. Go to your community meeting.

Community Meeting

In preparation for this week's meeting, you will have read and reflected upon each of the week's five Core Thoughts, recorded your thoughts and observations, and are ready to recite this week's memory verses to the group.

Next Steps

Each member of the community should take the next week to consider whether the Lord would like for them to form and lead a new ETL community. Here are some suggestions:

- Use the spiritual discipline of fasting to seek after the Lord's will regarding forming a new community.
- During your fast, ask the Lord to tell you who He would like in this new community.
- List ten people, who have not participated in ETL, as prospective members of the new community.

Name	Phone #
1.	
2.	
3.	
4.	
5.	
6.	
7.	
8.	
9.	
10.	

- Pray for the people on your list.
- Ask to meet with each of them to discuss their participation in an ETL community.
- Use the information from "About This Book" and "Preparing for the First Community Meeting" in Experience the Life, Book One to help you prepare to lead the new community.

AFTERWORD

Bill Hull

What have you learned about yourself? Did you become the kind of person who easily and naturally does the things Jesus did? I didn't ask you if you found Scripture memory easy and natural or keeping a journal or fasting or being silent or getting through a one-day retreat a piece of cake. Spiritual exercise is still exercise, and exercise works against the natural tendency to take it easy on yourself. People exercise in groups; they pay money for the needed structure because without support it usually doesn't last. We are all different; some people take to exercise and it becomes a habit. Others continue to exercise because they like the results. Still others quit exercise as soon as they can. So let me ask it another way: Have you enjoyed the benefits of spiritual exercise? Have you entered into God's presence, tasted His goodness, seen His beauty? Has your life taken on more of the fruit of the Holy Spirit? Have you found that living for others is the real secret to joy and purpose?

> It has been our purpose in EXPERIENCE THE LIFE to guide you into a life of humility, submission, obedience, and sacrifice, humility before God and others, submission to Christ and other members of His community, obedience to His commands, and sacrificial living for others. If you now understand this life, appreciate it, and sense that you are moving in that direction, then we are satisfied that we have done our part. In particular, if you open your Bible on a regular basis and read a passage and automatically enter into the process of 1. Read it; 2. Think it; 3. Pray it; and 4. Live it, then our part in your journey is fulfilled.

One of the EXPERIENCE THE LIFE lessons is to never go it alone. Just because the curriculum ends doesn't mean that supportive relationships end. The hallmark of a life of following Jesus is attachment to at least one other person to help keep it going. Go forward hand in hand, arm in arm, until we enter into His perfect presence. See you there!

ABOUT THE AUTHORS

BILL HULL's mission is to call the church to return to its disciple-making roots. He is a writer and discipleship evangelist calling the church to *choose the life*, a journey that Jesus called every disciple to pursue. This journey leads to a life of spiritual transformation and service. A veteran pastor, Bill has written ten books on this subject. In 1990 he founded T-NET International, a ministry devoted to transforming churches into disciple-making churches.

The core of Bill's writing is *Jesus Christ, Disciplemaker*; *The Disciple-Making Pastor*; and *The Disciple-Making Church*. He now spends his time helping leaders experience personal transformation so they can help transform their churches.

Bill and his wife, Jane, enjoy their not-so-quiet life, helping to raise their "highly energetic" grandchildren, in the beautiful Southern California sunshine.

PAUL MASCARELLA has served in local church ministry for more than twenty-five years as an associate pastor, minister of music, and worship director while holding an executive management position at a daily newspaper in Los Angeles, California. He is associate director of *Choose the Life Ministries*, where the abundance of his time and energy go to assisting churches as they embark on The *Choose the Life Journey*, and proceed forward with the EXPERIENCE THE LIFE series. He also serves on the board of directors for Bill Hull Ministries. He holds the Bachelor of Philosophy and Master of Theological Studies degrees.

Paul and his wife, Denise, reside in southern California.

ALSO BY
BILL HULL

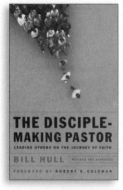
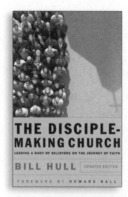
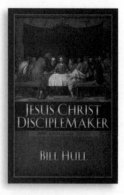

The Disciple-Making Pastor,
rev. & exp. ed.

The Disciple-Making Church,
updated ed.

Jesus Christ, Disciplemaker,
20th ann. ed.

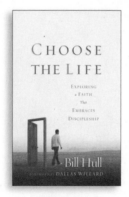

Choose the Life

Building High Commitment
in a Low-Commitment World

Ɍ Revell

BAKER PUBLISHING GROUP

www.bakerpublishinggroup.com

Change from ordinary
to Christlike.

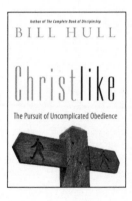

Christlike
Bill Hull
978-1-60006-694-8

To make a difference in the world, we need to become different ourselves. The final determination of whether or not a person is becoming Christlike is how we act in daily life. Bill Hull in *Christlike* will show you how to change outward actions by inner transformation through uncomplicated obedience.